Dear Friend,

I am pleased to send you this copy of *The Pursuit of Excellence* by Dr. George Sweeting, former president and chancellor of Moody Bible Institute. Dr. Sweeting has served as a pastor in several churches and has written numerous books.

This short but powerful book identifies nine character traits of influential Christians—plus the stories of people whose lives were marked by excellence, not mediocrity. God's Word urges believers to "*run with endurance the race that is set before us*" (Hebrews 12:1, ESV). To run with endurance is to run with strength to the very end, and I pray this book will inspire you to pursue excellence as a follower of the Lord Jesus Christ.

For more than 70 years, God has used the Billy Graham Evangelistic Association (BGEA) and friends like you to reach people all over the world with the Gospel. I'm so thankful for the ways He has worked—and what He will do in the years ahead.

If you represent one of the lives the Lord has touched, we would love to hear from you. Your story has the power to impact the lives of so many others. May God richly bless you.

Sincerely,

Franklin Graham
President & CEO

If you would like to know more about our ministry, please contact us:

IN THE U.S.:
Billy Graham Evangelistic Association
1 Billy Graham Parkway
Charlotte, NC 28201-0001
BillyGraham.org
info@bgea.org
Toll-free: 1-877-247-2426

IN CANADA:
Billy Graham Evangelistic
  Association of Canada
20 Hopewell Way NE
Calgary, AB T3J 5H5
BillyGraham.ca
Toll-free: 1-888-393-0003

THE PURSUIT OF EXCELLENCE

GEORGE SWEETING

MOODY PUBLISHERS

CHICAGO

This *Billy Graham Library Selection* special edition is published with
permission from Moody Publishers.

©1985, 2019 by
GEORGE SWEETING

Edited by Connor Sterchi
Interior design: Ragont Design
Cover design: Erik M. Peterson
Cover illustration of summit icon copyright © 2017 by Sudowoodo / istock (870978682). All rights reserved.
Photo of mountain climber by m wrona on Unsplash.
Author photo: Gail Sweeting

Library of Congress Cataloging-in-Publication Data

Names: Sweeting, George, 1924- author.
Title: The pursuit of excellence / George Sweeting.
Other titles: You can climb higher
Description: Chicago : Moody Publishers, [2019] | Original edition: You can climb higher. 1984 | Includes bibliographical references.
Identifiers: LCCN 2019003508 (print) | LCCN 2019010700 (ebook) | ISBN 9780802498069 () | ISBN 9780802419477
Subjects: LCSH: Christian life.
Classification: LCC BV 4501.3 (ebook) | LCC BV 4501.3 .S9446 2019 (print) | DDC 248.4--dc23
LC record available at https://lccn.loc.gov/2019003508

ISBN: 978-0-8024-1947-7
ISBN: 978-1-593-28710-8 (BGEA edition)

Moody Publishers
820 N. LaSalle Boulevard
Chicago, IL 60610

1 3 5 7 9 10 8 6 4 2

Printed in the United States of America

This book is gratefully dedicated to the Alumni of the Moody Bible Institute, past, present, and future, who are committed to the commission of Jesus, "Go into all the world and preach the gospel to all creation" (Mark 16:15 NIV).

Also, with great appreciation to our granddaughter, Erika Sweeting Dawson, who typed and shared insights for this manuscript.

CONTENTS

O Lord, our Lord, how excellent is thy name in all the earth! who hast set thy glory above the heavens.

Psalm 8:1 KJV

Let your light shine before others, that they may see your good deeds and glorify your Father in heaven.

Matthew 5:16 NIV

Some people have greatness thrust upon them. Very few have excellence thrust upon them. . . . They achieve it. They do not achieve it unwittingly by "doing what comes naturally," and they don't stumble into it in the course of amusing themselves. All excellence involves involves discipline and tenacity of purpose.

John W. Gardner, *Excellence*

Claiming the righteousness of Jesus Christ, I said, We're going to win! And we did.

C. Everett Koop

1

THE CHALLENGE TO EXCELLENCE

... that you may be able to discern what is best ...

Philippians 1:10 NIV

Run in such a way that you may win.

1 Corinthians 9:24 NASB

I do not run like someone running aimlessly ...

1 Corinthians 9:26 NIV

I press on toward the goal to win the prize for which
God has called me heavenward in Christ Jesus.

Philippians 3:14 NIV

Whoever I am or whatever I am doing,
some kind of excellence is within my reach.

John W. Gardner

The words of the ancient Oath of Hippocrates echoed through the halls of Cornell University as the medical class of 1941 recited their commitment to save human lives: "I will follow that method of treatment which, according to my ability and judgment, I consider for the benefit of my patients, and abstain from whatever is deleterious and mischievous."

Outwardly one young physician in the class seemed no different from the other bright students. Each one who wore the olive-green hood over their black cap and gown, signifying the medical degree, had a look of joy coupled with determination—joy in having completed the grueling years of preparation and determination to make that training serve themselves and others. But this young man had a different perspective from most; he believed in Jesus Christ as his Lord and intended to demonstrate his faith in his medical practice.

By 1953 he and a neurosurgeon combined their knowledge to develop a revolutionary procedure. They discovered how to drain water from the brain to prevent a condition that killed 90 percent of its victims before they were two years old. Babies once doomed to death could now live to become healthy children.

Over the next two decades this surgeon single-mindedly pursued his dream to establish the country's first neonatal intensive surgical-care unit and a total-care pediatric facility. In 1974, his pursuit of excellence led him to tackle an operation other doctors declared impossible. He separated the Rodriguez Siamese-twin girls, whose internal connections were multiple and complex. The day of that operation began, as always, with prayer and Bible reading. "A verse in Psalms, which said the Lord will support the righteous, became my help in time of need," the surgeon later told reporters. "Claiming the righteousness of Jesus Christ, I said, 'We're going to win!' And we did."[1]

Love characterized the surgeon's practice. He was known for his compassionate counseling to parents whose children were terminally ill. Most of all he loved children, including the deformed and unlovely ones. He could see beyond their brokenness to their unique spirits and the possibility of what they could become. But his dreams of healing hopelessly ill babies broke apart when the Supreme Court legalized abortion in 1973.

He called physicians back to the excellent way, the way espoused in the Hippocratic oath he had taken in 1941: "I will give no deadly medicine to anyone if asked, nor suggest any such counsel; furthermore, I will not give to a woman an instrument to produce an abortion.'"[2]

This pediatric surgeon, whom you may recognize as C. Everett Koop, knew he was making abortion advocates his bitter enemies. But he felt God calling him to take this stand.

In the fall of 1981, President Ronald Reagan recognized Koop's dedication to excellent medical care when he nominated him to be surgeon general for the United States. The surgeon's enemies bitterly opposed the nomination for nine long months.

But C. Everett Koop had always been a man of excellent character, so nothing in his past prevented his appointment to become surgeon general.

When the Senate confirmation hearings were finally held in November of 1981, testimony by twelve witnesses on his behalf made Koop's day on Capitol Hill a victory march.

In his book, *The Right to Live: The Right to Die*, Dr. Koop states, "Once there is the union of sperm and egg, and the twenty-three chromosomes of each are brought together. . . . That one cell with its forty-six chromosomes has all the DNA (deoxyribonucleic acid), the whole genetic code, and will, if not interrupted, make a human being just like you, with the potential for God-consciousness."[3] He asks a crucial question: "At what minute can one consider life to be worthless and the next minute consider the same life to be precious?"[4]

Later in his book, Dr. Koop quotes these words from a secular conference on abortion: "We can find no point in time between the union of sperm and egg and the birth of an infant at which point we can say this is not a human life."[5]

The New York Times reported Dr. Koop's death on February 25, 2013, in an article by Holcomb B. Noble titled, "C. Everett Koop, Forceful U.S. Surgeon General, Dies at 96." Dr. C. Everett Koop was totally committed to excellence.

Over my desk I have a poster of an Olympic runner winning a race. Underneath the victorious runner are the words of Paul the apostle: "Run in such a way that you may win" (1 Cor. 9:24 NASB). Average running rarely wins. Jesus challenged His followers to let their lights shine in such a way that their works would be seen and God would be glorified (Matt. 5:16). Mediocre shining will not penetrate the world around us. It was said of Paul and Barnabas that "they spoke so effectively that a great number . . . believed" (Acts 14:1 NIV). Passionless speaking convinces no one.

> It was said of Paul and Barnabas that "they spoke so effectively that a great number . . . believed" (Acts 14:1 NIV). Passionless speaking convinces no one.

The dictionary defines excellence as "superior, above the standard." When we speak of excellence, we speak of that which is choice, first rate, remarkably good!

A major problem in the pursuit of excellence is a lack of standards or confusion about what the standards are—and where they originate.

John W. Gardner reminds us,

Standards are contagious. They spread throughout an organization, a group or a society. If an organization or group cherishes high standards, the behavior of individuals who enter it is inevitably influenced. Similarly, if slovenliness infects a society, it is not easy for any member of that society to remain uninfluenced in his own behavior. With that grim fact in mind, one is bound to look with apprehension on many segments of our national life in which slovenliness has attacked like dry rot, eating away the solid timber.[6]

Just as one quality person motivates others to strive for excellence, so mediocrity spreads like a plague. George Eliot, speaking of Amos Barton, said, "It was not in his nature to be superlative in anything; unless, indeed, he was superlatively meddling, the quintessential extract of mediocrity."[7]

The dictionary defines mediocrity as "ordinary . . . neither good nor bad; barely adequate . . . poor; inferior."[8] Mediocrity is like playing five strings on a ten-stringed instrument. It is typing with five fingers and one eye rather than ten fingers and two eyes. It's a person with eagle talent thrashing his wings like a prairie chicken and flying no more than three feet off the ground. It is the individual with jet power doing push-cart work. Mediocrity is crawling on hands and knees when we were created to stand, walk, run, and mount up like an eagle and fly. Dare I say that scores of workers are mediocre? Many church leaders don't earn their salaries, and hundreds of teachers are painfully boring.

Speaking of standards, contemporary artist Charles Close said, "Art is a profession, without a measuring system. There is no way to tell if what I am doing is good . . . so what is quality? I don't know the answer."[9]

Psalm 8:1 states the source of all excellence. "O LORD, our Lord, how excellent is Your name in all the earth, who have set Your glory above the heavens!" According to the psalmist, the ultimate standard of excellence is found in God's name. His name represents all that God is. His name is the standard for excellence in heaven and here on earth.

God is holy, which means He is without parallel. He is merciful, almighty, just, unchanging, loving, and eternal. Not only is God excellent in His person, but He is excellent in His works (Ps. 19:1), and ways (2 Sam. 22:31), and will (Rom. 12:2).

The desire for excellence, contrary to the thinking of some, is not self-centered, but rather a divine, implanted desire to mimic God—to be as God is, and do what He does.

The National Bureau of Standards in Washington, DC, holds many standards of measurement, which other measurements must match throughout the nation. Just so, God's name, and a desire for excellence, contrary to the thinking of some, is not self-centered, but rather a divine, implanted desire to mimic God—to be as God is, and do what He does.

I like the way David the shepherd boy spoke of God's ways. "As for God, His way is perfect," David said. "And He makes my way perfect" (2 Sam. 22:31, 33). God's ways are not only perfect (complete), but He makes our way like His way.

Speaking of perfection is not speaking of perfectionism, which is impossible in this life. Rather, the challenge is to be and to do the best we are capable of being and doing.

God enables us to be like Him in spite of our sinfulness that leads us to tarnish God's image or to adopt the carnal desire for money, success, and prestige. The Israelites failed God in the wilderness, but we must not fail Him by turning to materialism, sex, alcohol, and drugs. God calls us to Himself and promises His power to enable us to be like Him.

God calls us to be 100 percent Christians. His resources can make us willing to stand with our friends and neighbors against the evils of our day. Ours need not be the day of the placid pulpit and the comfortable pew.

We must realize that our generation, which lauds the excellence of its scientific accomplishments, perceives God—and the validity of His existence—by our actions. One basis of our judgment before God is the quality of how we live: "The fire will test each one's work, of what sort it is" (1 Cor. 3:13).

God calls us to give our all. Excellence, by definition, means "the finest." It takes hard work and constant commitment, but we can excel. Many Christians seem to see how little they can

> Many Christians seem to see how little they can do and still remain God's servants. Yet we can learn from the dedication of the Old Testament Israelites who gave the Lord the firstfruits of their crops and the best of their flocks.

do and still remain God's servants, measuring their Christianity in teaspoonfuls of Bible reading, moments of prayer, occasional Sunday service, old suits or dresses for the missionaries, and just a little of their income for God's work. Yet we can learn from the dedication of the Old Testament Israelites who gave the Lord the firstfruits of their crops and the best of their flocks, which meant a lamb "without blemish" (Ex. 12:5).

David committed the sin of numbering the Hebrew people. The penalty was severe. His only hope of restoration was to make a sacrifice to show his repentance. One faithful citizen, named Ornan, offered David all he needed for his sacrifice—the oxen, the wood, and the wheat for a grain offering. It would have made David's work quite easy. But David refused the generous offer by saying, "I will not take what is yours for the LORD, nor offer burnt offerings with that which costs me nothing" (1 Chron. 21:24). Excellence is never cheap. It's costly. Constant care, serious preparation, and continual application are required. Excellence requires desire plus discipline plus determination.

I began my own pursuit of excellence during my student

days at the Moody Bible Institute. I sat under the teaching of quality professors. My compassion for a sinful world was kindled by some of this century's heroes of the faith who visited our campus. We were challenged to be our best and to give our best.

I encountered serious roadblocks along the way. During my senior year, the doctors discovered I had cancer. I underwent two immediate operation at Chicago's Swedish Covenant Hospital, followed by a series of radiation treatments. I faced the prospect of not living through that year. I walked through the valley of death.

But God in His mercy intervened and spared my life. Fellow students rallied to my side. With their prayers and help, I was able to complete the school year with honors. To me, graduation was my commissioning to the pursuit of excellence, which I have tried to follow to this day.

When I became president of Moody Bible Institute in 1971, I made the pursuit of excellence the theme of our administration. I placed on the front of my desk, where it could be seen easily, a bronze plaque with the word *Excellence* inscribed on it. I gave each member of my managerial staff a picture of Dwight L. Moody with *Excellence* written across it.

I knew that just saying, "We are committed to excellence" was not enough. So I searched the Scriptures for the qualities that lead to excellence. I found nine marks of Christian excellence: faith, character, action, single-mindedness, love, suffering, prayer, wisdom, and staying power. These marks can be seen throughout the Bible, particularly in Matthew 5, Galatians

5, and James 3:17–18. These qualities blended together give us a portrait of what God is like. Since God is excellent, these same characteristics mark out what we ought to pursue. Chapters 2 through 10 will examine each of these marks of excellence and tell how to achieve them.

I also studied the lives of quality people. They displayed these same traits, as you will see particularly in chapters 11, 12, and 13. Finally, I questioned Christian educators and leaders and discovered a consensus among them. Each felt that excellence is impossible apart from a God-like character.

I began this chapter with a quotation from John W. Gardner: "Whoever I am or whatever I am doing, some kind of excellence is within my reach." The pursuit of excellence is not just for a privileged few, like C. Everett Koop. Nor is excellence reserved for the elite or genius. It is for you—whoever you are, wherever you are, whatever you do.

Today many people feel the roles of wife and mother are mediocre and mundane. I fervently reject this attitude. My wife excels as a mother and wife. For years she has taken time to listen to our children's fears and feelings of inadequacy, as well as to their dreams. She has always been there to sympathize, to offer an encouraging word at the right time, to make the children feel comfortable with who they are and what they have done—and what they hope to achieve. It is she, more than I, who set their feet on the road to do God's will. Both of us have given our best to be with them each step of their journey.

You do not have to be the surgeon general or an outstanding business person or a well-known writer to achieve excellence. God knows many people who have achieved excellence that you and I have never heard about. It is the quality of what you are and do that counts. Join me in this adventure to make spiritual excellence part of your life. I promise that if you do, it will change you—and the world around you.

. . . faith comes from hearing the message, and the message is heard through the word about Christ.

Romans 10:17 NIV

But when you ask, you must believe and not doubt, because the one who doubts is like a wave of the sea, blown and tossed by the wind.

James 1:6 NIV

We are what we are because of what we do with our opportunities.

Every problem is a chance to experience God's supernatural power.

2

FAITH—THE POWER TO MOVE MOUNTAINS

"Have faith in God," Jesus answered. "Truly I tell you, if anyone says to this mountain, 'Go, throw yourself into the sea,' and does not doubt in their heart but believes that what they say will happen, it will be done for them."

Mark 11:22-23 NIV

. . . without faith it is impossible to please Him.

Hebrews 11:6

My dad's life wasn't easy. He arrived in the United States in 1923 as a Scottish stonemason. Not long after that, America experienced the trauma of the Great Depression. The stock market crashed, and in the panic that followed, many of the leading businessmen in the country committed suicide.

For about five years, little building went on in the United States. My father couldn't find work for more than half of those years. We all took any job we could find. I can remember as a young boy selling magazines and delivering milk every Friday night and all day Saturday for a dollar a day. Our family made paper flowers and sold them door-to-door, just to get a quarter, fifty cents, or a dollar. My parents put our house up for sale because we could not make the mortgage payments.

As a family we found strength to keep going because we fully believed the Lord was in complete control, all the time, even in poverty and want. Mother would occasionally remind us, "God is too good to be unkind and too wise to make a mistake." During our daily family devotions, we found unity and great faith as we identified with the humiliation and poverty of the children of Israel in their desert wanderings—and their ultimate possession of the Promised Land.

Eventually, building resumed. My dad got a job laying bricks and went on to lead a significant company. But without his faith in God, without our family's faith in God, we never could have withstood the hard times of the Depression.

All of life is a journey, and each person is a pilgrim. Everyone is faced with decisions that determine life's outcome. The basic decision everyone must make is: Will I believe in God and receive Jesus Christ as my personal Savior?

Excellence can never be achieved without the Lord. Novelist Anthony Burgess described excellence in this way: "There's a whiff of morality around it. . . . The 'heavenward' connotation is, I think, inseparable from the term. . . . If God exists, then He is excellent and by extension His works are excellent, too."[1]

WE START BY FAITH

The first step in achieving excellence is to answer this basic question positively, "Yes, I believe Jesus Christ is God's provision for my sins." Our first parents, Adam and Eve, were made in God's image and given dominion over all creation, but that perfect image was defaced by their disobedience. Instead of excelling, they forfeited dominion over creation and even dominion over themselves. The good news of the gospel is that through Christ we can be reborn.

Because of Christ's death and resurrection we can in this life, here and now, be "more than conquerors" (Rom. 8:37 NIV) —literally, "overwhelmingly conquerors." Excellence is not just pie in the sky; it's God's plan for each Christian now.

Many people in our world believe only in what they can see, touch, and feel. Christians look beyond the physical and see the reality of a God who exists and cares about this world and about each individual in it. You. Me. Our children.

Sometimes trusting the Lord seems difficult. But think of the times you actually exercise faith when you have little reason to do so. Have you ever been in a small, prop airplane that seats eight passengers? It's as if you are sitting on a chair in the middle of the sky. Even if you fly in a jet, the aluminum shell of the planes is all that separates you from open space—and probable death if the plane goes down. You're really putting a lot of faith in the airplane and the pilot every time you fly.

After all, you are not able to watch the mechanics check the plane for malfunctions before takeoff. You can't stand beside the workers who assembled the plane or the engineers who designed it. Certainly you have no proof of the pilot's ability. You just have faith that the crew are professional, and you trust your life to them. In the same way, you can trust your life fully to an all-powerful, loving God.

When it comes right down to it, little in this world is worthy of our complete trust. The stockholder who depends upon his stocks to help him succeed often learns that stocks go down as often—or more frequently—than up. The miser who stores her money in the bank "for a rainy day" can be caught in a bank closure.

Long ago, I made the decision to put my faith in the Lord Jesus Christ rather than in the visible things of this world. Have you welcomed Jesus Christ into your life so that He can live His life in you? Once you do, you have begun to walk the path to excellence. Excellence begins with a decision to receive Jesus as Savior and Lord.

The next decision of life is, Shall I hold onto this faith, or shall I doubt? Am I willing to trust God no matter how impossible the situation seems? Am I willing to trust God no matter how long my difficulties continue? You can defeat doubt, through the Lord Jesus Christ, when it attacks your faith and when you face the inevitable troubles of life.

WE CONTINUE BY FAITH

The great patriarchs cited for their faith in Hebrews 11 believed in God despite difficult and impossible situations. Abraham believed God's promise that he would be the father of many nations, even when he and Sarah reached their twilight years without children. The world said Sarah was barren, but Abraham believed God!

Faith is trusting God when there is no reason to. Faith is trusting God in the face of opposition. When the Israelites finally arrived at the border town of Kadesh Barnea and were within reach of the Promised Land, they faced their biggest challenge. Would they advance and take the land by faith, or would they choose to doubt?

The Israelites faced an impossible situation. Ten of the twelve spies reported, "The cities are fortified and very large. . . . We are not able to go up against the people, for they are stronger than we. . . . There we saw the giants . . . and we were like grasshoppers in our own sight, and so we were in their sight" (Num. 13:28, 31, 33).

There was a lot of truth in what the ten spies said. The cities were walled, and the Anaks were people of unusual stature; they would not give up without a fight. The ten spies saw real problems, a seemingly impossible situation, but they failed to include God in the picture.

Pandemonium followed their faithless report, the same fear and confusion that sometimes invade our lives when things are at their worst. The doubt of these ten unbelieving men became infectious and spread like wildfire. But Caleb and Joshua, the other two of the twelve spies, chose to have faith despite the situation. Caleb said, "Let us go up at once and take possession, for we are well able to overcome it" (Num. 13:30). "Let us go up at once," not, "Let's train our soldiers and plan for several months." These two men thought the Israelites could take the land immediately.

How could there be two such different reports? Why do some excel and others fail? Because Caleb and Joshua—and thousands of people like them today—had the element of faith. They put God in the picture. The Israelites saw only the walled cities and the giants. Caleb and Joshua saw beyond the visible to the invisible reality of God. They knew that He was active in their world just as He walked with their forefathers—Abraham, Isaac, and Jacob. They refused to doubt God. Why not follow their example? Why not trust God for the impossible? You, too, will excel as you continue by faith.

We start by faith, and we must continue by faith. The rallying cry of the Reformation was, "The just shall live by faith" (Rom. 1:17). Commitment to Jesus Christ is the first step of faith. Trusting God for the impossible is the second. The third is the ability to finish by faith no matter how long and how difficult times are.

WE FINISH BY FAITH

Too often we have faith for the short run but not for the long haul. We have enough faith to make it through the first few months of crisis—a job loss or a critical illness in the family—but we give up and become desperate by the fourth or fifth month.

It is difficult to keep going when you're worried about whether your spouse or child will live or die. No matter how hard you try to displace your doubts—What if he/she should die or become handicapped for life? What would I do?—they rise to the surface.

God calls us to conquer such panic, which is really doubt grown larger and larger until it turns into fear. "Fear not, for I am with you," God promises now, just as He promised Caleb and Isaiah in the Old Testament and Christ's apostles in the New Testament. As Paul said, "If God is for us, who can be against us?" (Rom. 8:31). I have found that memorizing these verses helped me experience the strength that comes from understanding and believing the promises of God.

The greatest barrier to a faith that leads to excellence is the tendency to quit. I was reminded of this recently when I rented a car to travel to a small town north of Indianapolis.

My friend, whom I have every reason to trust, had given me directions over the phone. I chose to take Route 70 as my friend had instructed, rather than Interstate 465, which the rental agent told me to take. My friend had explained that 70 went straight across the city and ran into 465, which circled the city and would add extra miles to my trip. However, as ten, then fifteen, then twenty-five minutes went by and there was still no sight of Interstate 465, I began to doubt.

Had I heard my friend correctly?

Highways began to turn off to Louisville, then to Columbus, Ohio. My friend had admitted that she didn't get to the city much, and, after all, she was originally from Michigan, not Indiana. Maybe her way wasn't right.

I finally gave up and turned off the highway to ask for directions. As usual, I wished I had trusted my friend's directions just a little longer. Only a few miles ahead, Interstate 465 did join Route 70. I had avoided circling the city by taking Route 70. I had some faith—but not quite enough.

Humans are enigmas. At times we seem to trust like children. At other times we doubt too easily, as I did when I tried to follow my friend's directions in a strange town, which is not too different from following God's directions on this strange planet called Earth.

What mistakes did I make?

First, I wondered if I had understood my friend properly. This nagging feeling of doubt is similar to the querying of false theology: "Did God really say that? Does He really mean that? Certainly the creation story and Noah and the Flood are just allegories. And while we're thinking about it, we all know that miracles in the Bible can be explained by natural phenomena. Furthermore, such miracles don't happen today; they were just for biblical times." Slowly doubt creeps in and destroys faith because we do not fully trust God and His Word in Scripture.

Second, I questioned my friend's ability. We need to know and believe that God is able. Abraham had so much faith in God's power that he believed God was able to raise Isaac from the dead (see Heb. 11:19).

Caleb knew God had said, "Possess the land." Doubt said, "Nevertheless, we can't." Caleb believed so strongly in God's power that there was no room in his life for the word *nevertheless*. Unfortunately, we often add this word to the promise, "I can do all things through Christ" (Phil. 4:13).

> Not once, not twice, but six times in the Bible we read that Caleb "wholly followed the Lord." That is the secret of Caleb's pursuit of excellence.

When we doubt, we cut ourselves off from His help. We are doomed to failure because God can't help us. What happened to the spies who doubted and regarded themselves as grasshoppers? They were killed by the plague. That entire generation wandered in the wilderness for forty years and died there. It was the world's longest funeral march—all because of doubt and unbelief. What happened to Caleb and Joshua? They achieved excellence.

Not once, not twice, but six times in the Bible we read that Caleb "wholly followed the LORD" (see Num. 32:11–12; Deut. 1:36; Josh. 14:8–9, 14). That is the secret of Caleb's pursuit of excellence. He followed God no matter what. He did not allow himself to doubt.

Finally, I asked if my friend's way was really right. That is the ultimate question of doubt. It turns doubt into rejection of God, His commandments, and His way of life. We may say, "Christianity doesn't work today. It was okay for the simple people of an agrarian society, but it is not for those who live in a technical age. Only people who can't handle their own problems look to God for help." We may turn our backs on God and rely on science, psychology, or some new philosophical theory. Skepticism often leads to atheism.

Without faith, we cannot achieve excellence. The Christian life begins by faith in Jesus Christ (see Eph. 2:8–9), and it must continue by faith. In fact, without faith, "it is impossible to please God" (Heb. 11:6 NIV). I can build a house without faith. I can marry without faith. It is possible to earn a million dollars without faith. But it is impossible to please God without faith. Even the Greek word for "man," *anthropos* ("the up-looking one"), indicated that we must look up to God for everything.

The apostle Paul summarized his life just before he was martyred: "I have fought the good fight, I have finished the race, I have kept the faith" (2 Tim. 4:7). Of everything Paul accomplished in his life, these three things he considered the most important. The greatest challenge of the Christian life is to keep the faith "until the day of Christ Jesus" (Phil. 1:6 NASB).

How is it with you? Do you face a situation that seems impossible, a Kadesh Barnea that could change the whole course of your future? Each person at some time or other faces a Kadesh Barnea.

The giants you fight may not seem spectacular. Perhaps you need to display greater faith in your marriage partner. Nothing undercuts a marriage more than a lack of faith. Maybe you've given up on yourself. Always remember that God made you, redeemed you, and is enthusiastically for you (see Rom. 8:31). God is not neutral toward you. He is positively for you!

Don't be misled by the circumstances or awed by the difficulties of life. They are not of primary importance. Remember Caleb's secret. It is your faith in God, His will, and His faithfulness that count.

Caleb won the battles of life because he first won the inner battle of faith, obedience, and commitment to God in his own heart. He did not allow himself to doubt. That was his real secret, and it must be ours as well if we wish to pursue biblical excellence.

Many Americans may not recognize the name of William Cameron Townsend, but many know of the work of the Wycliffe Bible Translators, who have translated the New Testament into more than two hundred native languages throughout the world. Townsend's favorite song was:

Faith, mighty faith, the promise sees,
And looks to that alone.

Laughs at impossibilities
And cries, It shall be done!

The song has become a part of the Wycliffe heritage. In fact, one of the five principles of the Wycliffe organization is, "We trust God for the impossible."

What a motto! Uncle Cam and Wycliffe have shown what a mighty faith can do for one man or for one organization. More than five thousand translators and missionaries now working in over ninety-three countries. All because one man had faith that God could do the impossible!

Caleb excelled because he had faith, which is the first and most important step in the Christian's pursuit of excellence. He went into the Promised Land and settled near Hebron, the mountainous part of the country where lived those giantlike people who frightened the other spies.

Caleb was still accomplishing the impossible at an age when many give up and retire. When Caleb was eighty-five years old, he asked the Lord to allow him to remove the giants so he might claim the mountain for his possession. "As yet I am as strong this day as on the day that Moses sent me; just as my strength was then, so now is my strength for war. . . . Therefore, give me this mountain" (Josh. 14:11–12). Even though he was a senior, Caleb directed the battle against the giants and drove them out. Caleb possessed a spirit of victory. His attitude for a lifetime was "Give me this mountain!" It can be yours, too, if you choose to be a person of great faith in God!

Character is the sum and total of a person's choices.

P. B. Fitzwater

Character is what [you are] in the dark.

D. L. Moody

Now Joseph was well-built and handsome, and after a while his master's wife took notice of Joseph and said, "Come to bed with me!" But he refused.

Genesis 39:6–8 NIV

Humility is as scarce as an albino robin.

A. W. Tozer

3

CHARACTER—THE PURITY TO SERVE

Above all else, guard your heart, everything you do flows from it.

Proverbs 4:23 NIV

Clothe yourself with the Lord Jesus Christ, and do not think about how to gratify the desires of the flesh.

Romans 13:14 NIV

"These are the ones I look on with favor: those who are humble and contrite in spirit, and who tremble at my word."

Isaiah 66:2 NIV

One long line of gravestones in the cemetery of Princeton University is called "President's Row." It includes the graves of this renowned school's presidents and their families. The inscription on one stone reads: "Aaron Burr, A Colonel in the Army of the Revolution, Vice President of the United States from 1801 to 1805." Near his grave are those of his pious father, the Reverend Aaron Burr, who was the second president of Princeton, and of his famous grandfather, Jonathan Edwards, theologian and evangelist.

Aaron Burr had all that heredity and religious training could give a person. Burr's college record shows that he was unsurpassed in brilliance and accomplishment. Ability of mind and personality and a strong will were abundant. But what about character?

His life answers this question only too well. Burr so distinguished himself in the early years of the Revolutionary War that he was placed on General George Washington's staff. But he was soon transferred because of differences with his superior.

He saved a whole brigade from capture during their retreat from Long Island, but he defied orders to do so.

After the war, his legal brilliance was recognized. He was elected to the New York State Assembly and later was appointed attorney general of the state of New York. At the age of thirty-five he was elected to the United States Senate. Burr became such a power among Democratic-Republicans of the North that in 1800 he was nominated as vice president on the Jefferson ticket.

In fact, his personal canvassing and admirable organization were responsible for a Democratic victory in New York. But to accomplish this success he organized the infamous Tammany Society, which controlled New York politics for years through its notoriously illegal activities.

Through a blunder in the electoral process, Burr received as many electoral votes as Jefferson, which threw the final decision into the House of Representatives, even though Burr had been slated as the vice presidential candidate.

Then began the historic feud between Burr and Alexander Hamilton. Hamilton's determined opposition to Burr finally led to Jefferson's election. But rumors said that Burr connived to wrest the presidency from his chief during this time, so Jefferson never trusted him.

When Burr tried to retrieve his political fortunes by running for governor of New York in 1804, Hamilton again threw his influence against him as a "dangerous" man of whom he "could detail . . . a still more despicable opinion." Embittered by his defeat, Burr demanded an explanation of these words, Hamilton quibbled further, and Burr challenged him to the famous duel.

The shot that killed Hamilton indirectly killed Burr. He became an outcast from his country's social and political life. Bereft of his moorings, he disappeared to the western frontier. But he returned to the East with a plan to lead a colony of settlers to land he had purchased in Louisiana and perhaps to found a new state. He even talked about leading an expedition to Mexico, if the possible war with Spain materialized, so that he could win that country for the United States—or for himself. No one was really sure.

Burr was accused of trying to create a new republic in the Southwest, and in early 1807, he was tried for treason. Even though he was later exonerated, public opinion never recognized his innocence. He fled to Europe, where he wandered from country to country, living an immoral life in pathetic circumstances on borrowed funds. When he was evicted from England, he visited France, only to be scorned by Napoleon.

Eventually Aaron Burr returned to New York in disguise so that no one aboard the ship would recognize him. He resumed his practice of law but had little success for the next twenty-two years. He lived out his loneliness until death claimed him.

He was then carried to Princeton and buried near his good father and grandfather.[1]

This is the story of one of the brightest men who ever graduated from Princeton. But Burr never controlled the shadowy side of his character. His life was a continuous struggle between the good and evil within him, a war that is common to all of us. Aaron Burr had a chance for excellence but ended up so far, far away from it. His fatal flaw was his defective character. Without a good character, a person can never achieve excellence.

> Without a good character, a person can never achieve excellence. Character can be either good or bad, and such is the dilemma of life. Who will we be?

One of my professors defined character as "the sum and total of a person's choices." I like this definition since the word itself is morally neutral. Character can be either good or bad, and such is the dilemma of life. Who will we be?

Prolific writer Oscar Wilde confessed, "I let myself be lured into long spells of senseless and sensual ease. . . . Tired of being on the heights, I deliberately went to the depths in search for new sensation. . . . I grew careless of the lives of others. . . . I forgot that every little action of the common day makes or unmakes character, and that therefore what one has done in the secret chamber, one has some day to cry aloud from the house-top. I ceased to be lord over myself. I was no longer the captain of my soul, and did not know it. I allowed pleasure to dominate me. I ended in horrible disgrace."[2]

Unfortunately, today's emphasis is on doing rather than being. The call is for action, with little attention to character. But being must come first. We must know who we are before we can excel.

Remember your high school yearbook? You were asked to write out your life's ambitions. What do you want to do? Some answered:

> **Today's emphasis is on doing rather than being. But being must come first. We must know who we are before we can excel.**

Travel the world.
Reach the highest rung of the ladder of success.
Play professional baseball.
Be a rich movie star.

You might add your own answer to this list. Some of these were probably written in haste—and a few in jest. But the accent was clearly on doing rather than being.

There is nothing wrong with action. In fact, the next chapter discusses the importance of action. But it is more necessary to decide what to be than what to do.

In the Old Testament, Joseph was called a "dreamer" by his brothers, but his expansive dreams came true. Why? Joseph decided who he was before he decided what he would do, and he lived out his vision in everything he did. Joseph was a man of character. A look at his life shows us the attributes of a godly character: purity, honesty, humility, and faithfulness. Success does not depend on the dreams we dream but on the choices we make.

JOSEPH WAS PURE

Obviously, Joseph chose to be pure. His decisions were guided by his faith in God, which led him to follow God's commandments. Character always follows faith; it is a fruit of our desire to please God. Joseph proved his character in the choices he made each day. When the wife of Potiphar, the officer who bought Joseph as a slave, saw how handsome he was and how well he managed his master's business concerns, she boldly invited him, "Lie with me."

> Joseph decided who he was before he decided what he would do, and he lived out his vision in everything he did.

Joseph refused. It would have been easy for him to rationalize, I am the servant, and she is the employer. Instead, he answered, "How then can I do this great wickedness, and sin against God?" Joseph knew he was God's child, called to serve only Him. His desire to please God was more important than any lust he might have felt.

Potiphar's wife would not be put off. One day she arranged for the servants to be away. When Joseph came into the house, she caught him by his garment, saying, "Lie with me."

But he "left his garment in her hand, and fled and ran outside" (Gen. 39:12). The flesh is sometimes so powerful and deceitful that only a desperate dash will deliver us. We need to know when that time is.

The Scriptures warn us to "flee . . . youthful lusts" (2 Tim. 2:22). That's exactly what Joseph did. Perhaps you work for someone who expects moral compromises from you. If you are not able to resist his or her influence, don't hang around and invite trouble. If you must quit your job, then do so. God is more concerned about your character than your position in life.

All sin starts in the mind. If you struggle with lust, don't view provocative TV shows, magazines, or websites. Put safeguards and accountability in place to govern your internet and smartphone use. You can have the mind and the power of Christ (see 1 Cor. 2:16; Phil. 4:13); therefore you don't have to yield to temptations.

Unfortunately, saying no to temptation has gone out of style, and "doing what comes naturally" has become popular. Some people allow themselves to be tempted by the sin Joseph rejected. Married men and women lust after those who seem younger, or more talented, or better-looking than their spouses. Others may continually give in to violent and quick tempers, which may lead to child or spouse abuse. Christians rarely admit to the darker side of their characters.

Sin begins like a small, innocent, enchanting breeze—a few too many glances at an attractive person, the opportunity to see that person a few too many times. But those compromises escalate to tornado proportions. Sin destroys character.

It amazes me that some of us are so surprised by the

> Sin begins like a small, innocent, enchanting breeze. But those compromises escalate to tornado proportions. Sin destroys character.

natural weakness of our wills. We think that because we are Christians, temptation should be easy for us to avoid. But that's not what Jesus said. Knowing that we are bound by our humanity, He urged us to watch and pray. He challenged us to a constant vision of who we are and a constant vigilance to maintain that vision. Vance Havner used to remind us that "no one is ever safe 'til they're home in heaven."

JOSEPH WAS HONEST

Joseph chose to be honest. Integrity is vital to excellent character. "His word is his bond" is a first-rate compliment about anyone. Hypocrisy and deceit kill excellence.

Proverbs 11:3 sets out the importance of this quality: "The integrity of the upright will guide them, but the perversity of the unfaithful will destroy them." Simply put, honesty builds, but dishonesty destroys.

For many years, Dr. Madison Sarratt taught mathematics at Vanderbilt University. Before giving exams, he would say something like this: "Today I am giving two examinations, one in trigonometry and the other in honesty. I hope you will pass them both. If you must fail one, fail trigonometry. There are many good people in the world who can't pass trigonometry, but there are no good people who cannot pass the examination of honesty."[3]

Honesty is the name of the game. The writer of Proverbs warned, "Keep your heart with all diligence, for out of it spring the issues of life" (Prov. 4:23). Of course, here the word *heart* means more than the pump that keeps your blood circulating. It speaks of the inner you, known only to yourself and to God.

Many people have been noted for their integrity. As food administrator for the Allies during World War I, Herbert Hoover handled gigantic sums of money without any question. Franklin Lane, Hoover's biographer, wrote:

> The money (a total of twelve million dollars a month) was simply sent to him, Herbert C. Hoover. Those hundreds of millions passing constantly through his personal bank-account were guarded by nothing but his own integrity, which to all the governments of Europe was a security as sound as a government bond.[4]

To a world that has seen an abundance of scandals, such integrity may seem impossible, but it isn't. Excellent character begins with little choices. Did the sales clerk give you too much change? Do you keep it or return it? Maybe you have an office in your home, a desk and some files in a corner of a room. Do you take the entire room off your income tax, or do you claim the portion of space the equipment actually occupies? Each small decision you make, each time you bend the truth a little to benefit yourself, establishes a pattern—one that is difficult to break.

Joseph also determined to be humble; he was content with his position. He never tried to manipulate his way into a higher spot. Instead, he decided to serve to the best of his ability in whatever position he held. Genesis 38:8 speaks volumes: "And Joseph found grace in his sight, and he served him." Over the years, Joseph served Jacob, he served Potiphar, he served the keeper of the prison, he served the pharaoh—but most of all, he served God. The key to his excellent character was the strength of his humble service. God alone elevated Joseph!

You, too, can be a servant in your home, in your relationships with others, and in your job. Is there any task too lowly for you? Joseph would answer no. Does your employer see your true character through the quality of your work? Does he or she trust you with both small and large tasks? When you're asked to perform menial duties, do you devote the same amount of time and energy that you would to a greater responsibility?

Jesus set the greatest example in the way He ministered to others, shown most symbolically during the Passover feast. Jesus knew that He was God, that He was supreme, and that He was the number one leader. Yet He rose from supper, poured water into a basin, and began to wash the disciples' feet and to wipe them with a towel. Jesus Christ, the God-Man, served humbly. We are all called to belong to the "order of the towel."

JOSEPH WAS FAITHFUL

Joseph chose to be faithful. What was Joseph's reward for fleeing the advance of Potiphar's wife? He was thrown into prison, not a reward by anyone's standards. Yet Joseph remained faithful to God's laws. Others might have tried to manipulate a way out of prison by bribing the guards for special favors. They might have thought, *Following God's ways doesn't work. What have I gained by doing what's right?* They might have abandoned God. Joseph remained faithful to God and faithful to his vision to be what God wanted him to be.

We, too, must remain true to our dream of who we are as sons and daughters of Christ. "No magnificent building ever grew up by a miracle," said J. R. Miller in *The Building of Character*. "Stone by stone it rose, each block laid in its place by toil and effort. 'You cannot dream yourself into a character, you must hammer and forge yourself one.'"[5] Faithfulness is essential to an upright character.

Bitterness and unforgiveness are barriers to faithfulness. When Joseph's brothers came to Egypt to plead for food, Joseph had the perfect opportunity for revenge. He could have allowed them to starve to death. He could have

> **Joseph's level of success may be unattainable for most of us, but his quality of character is not.**

claimed an eye for an eye, a tooth for a tooth. Instead, Joseph forgave them. He looked at them, turned away, and wept.

Bitterness and unforgiveness obstruct our communion with God. We must have forgiving hearts. We may rationalize that we have good reasons to be bitter about matters, but we're told to leave vengeance with God. A truly forgiving person weeps at the folly of another's action.

Joseph's level of success may be unattainable for most of us, but his quality of character is not. He faced nothing in his spiritual life that will not be faced by each of us. What was the secret of Joseph's godly character? First, Joseph decided who he was as a child of God and how he could achieve that vision. Then he determined to be God's man. He chose to be pure. He determined to be honest, humble, and faithful because his overwhelming desire was to please God, to serve only Him.

What about you? Do you love Jesus Christ enough to deny your natural tendencies and achieve excellence? The choices of your life record your love for Him. Does your story read like Joseph's? If it does, you are on the road to excellence!

It is difficult to steer a parked car . . . so get moving.

Henrietta Mears

. . . choose for yourselves this day whom you will serve. . . .

Joshua 24:15 NIV

The road marked "Tomorrow" leads to the town called "Never"!

ACTION—THE COMMITMENT TO MAKE A DIFFERENCE

Whatever your hand finds to do, do it with all your might.

Ecclesiastes 9:10 NIV

Do not merely listen to the word, and
so deceive yourselves. Do what it says.

James 1:22 NIV

Energy is the dynamo, the power plant of personality,
the driving force upon which all other traits depend.
It is the Alpha but not the Omega of leadership.

E. S. Bogardus

After observing thousands of college students throughout many decades, I have discovered a common trait that marks those who excel: a burning desire that lasts for a lifetime.

Let me tell you the story of John Beekman, a Moody Bible Institute student who had such a desire. Shortly after entering school, John expressed concern for people who had no written copy of the Scriptures. That concern grew into an intense desire to do something about it.

John faced a major problem, one that would have stopped most of us: he had been born with a defective heart. When he applied to serve as a chaplain's assistant in the army, the doctors classified him 4F, a classification given to a new US military registrant indicating that he or she is "not acceptable for service in the Armed Forces" due to medical, dental, or other reasons.

At first he assumed 4F in the army meant 4F for missionary work, too. Certainly many people with a handicap of this kind would have dismissed missionary service as impossible, but not John.

Instead, he sought the advice of Dr. Titus Johnson, Moody's resident physician, who confirmed the army doctor's diagnosis. "You definitely have a heart and circulatory problem. I'm not a specialist, you understand, but my prognosis is that you may not live past forty."

Without a moment's hesitation, Johnson, himself a former missionary, said, "John, if the Lord wants you on the mission field, He'll get you there. And if I were you, I would much rather spend ten years of dedicated life on the mission field where there are many who have not yet heard the gospel message, than choose to stay here in the States and perhaps live a longer life ministering among people who have heard it many times already."

"Thanks," John replied. "That's all I needed to hear."

In that moment, John's desire turned into a commitment to do missionary work.[1]

COMMITMENT

A heartfelt commitment, like that of John Beekman, is necessary to excellence. We can "fall in love," but we don't "fall into excellence." Only the strength of a firm commitment can overcome the mud of everyday life. It changes what could be a fleeting emotion into the continuous effort to do our very best in everything we do today, tomorrow, next year, and ten years from now. Excellence is more than a wish; it's a pursuit that never stops.

People sometimes speak of experiencing an identity crisis. Sometimes they express the desire for time to get away to discover who they are and their reasons for continuing on. John Beekman never suffered such a crisis. Identity is found in commitment.

Where did commitment take John Beekman? It carried him to the land of Chiapas, the home of the Chol Indians in southern Mexico, near the Guatemalan border. There the terrain is rugged. Precipitous gorges are split by swift rivers. When John and his wife, Elaine, were there in 1947, fourteen different Indian tribes speaking fifteen dialects struggled to survive in the primitive environment. There were no roads, no telephones, no hospitals, and no doctors. Just disease, witchcraft, and drunkenness.

> A deeply rooted commitment leads to action that makes a difference in our own lives and in the lives of others.

John's commitment was translated into a struggle to survive and to serve. He and his wife trudged the mountainous trails between villages and sloshed through the mud on foot, efforts that often exhausted John. But he refused to allow his weak and erratically beating heart to stop him. Day after day he walked the territory, learning the Indians' language and superstitions.

A deeply rooted commitment leads to action that makes a difference in our own lives and in the lives of others. Scripture challenges us to act. We must be "doers of the word, and not hearers only." In turn, God promises that "a doer of the word . . . will be blessed in what he does" (James 1:22, 25).

ACTION

In their book *In Search of Excellence*, Thomas J. Peters and Robert H. Waterman suggest eight qualities that are characteristic of excellent companies in the United States. The first is "a bias for action," which Peters and Waterman describe as a tendency to act rather than to remain passive.

The authors use phrases like "do it," "fix it," and "try it," and they state that "chaotic action is preferable to orderly inaction." The excellent companies, we are told, give considerable time and money to experimentation. They are not afraid to try. On the other hand, the mediocre companies prefer analysis and debate; they appear to be paralyzed by fear of failure or change. They have a tendency to be so thorough that their work is boring. The authors believe the excellent companies' successes appear to be aligned closely with their ability to experiment quickly and almost endlessly.[2]

Most of us learn by doing. Few of us studied a manual to learn how to row a boat or play baseball or ride a bike. Instead, we learned by trying, observing, and practicing. Peters and Waterman suggest there is "no magic in the experiment." It is "simply a tiny completed action, a manageable test that helps you learn something, just as in high-school chemistry."[3]

Believe it or not, the experiment can fail and still succeed. One company mentioned by Peters and Waterman, Ore-Ida, a successful frozen foods subsidiary of Heinz, shoots off a cannon to celebrate the moment when "a perfect failure" occurs.[4] This concept arises from the recognition that all research and development is risky and that the only way to succeed is to try and try again.

Successful individuals have naturally followed this principle. Before he had successfully invented the incandescent lightbulb, Thomas Edison was taunted by someone who said, "Isn't it a shame that with the tremendous amount of work you have done you haven't been able to get any results?"

"Results!" responded Edison. "Why, man, I have gotten a lot of results! I know several thousand things that won't work."[5]

John Beekman had to be willing to experiment to achieve excellence. For a year, he was unable to reach the Indians because of their belief in spirits. He tried different approaches and failed each time. Finally, he realized that he could use their belief to help the Chols understand Christianity. "The witch doctor is right," he told them. "You can be indwelt by spirits. . . . [But I] have come to tell [you] about a Spirit more powerful than all the witch doctor's spirits put together. . . . This Spirit is God's Spirit! And he wants to live in the hearts of all men everywhere."[6]

Using this approach and the energy of the boy preachers he trained, John began to succeed. Throughout the region, Indians made a commitment to Christ as their Savior and Lord.

But the new converts had little guidance to help their faith grow. The gospel of Mark had been translated into Chol, but the Indians couldn't seem to understand it. Again, John had to experiment. He decided to translate a few Old Testament stories himself, even though he had been trained as a general Wycliffe worker with an emphasis on literacy and church organization.

John was willing to try a revolutionary approach. Instead of the literal, word-by-word, clause-by-clause procedure that had been used to translate the gospel of Mark, he brought together a small group of Chol men to help him convey the overall meaning of the Bible stories.

The Chols loved the stories. Soon the small community of Christians began to grow. John became determined to give the Indians a Bible in their own language. This became his lifetime passion and pursuit.

But many worthwhile goals have been blocked by excuses. Benjamin Franklin is attributed with saying, "He that is good for making excuses, is seldom good for anything else."

EXCUSES

There is a big difference between a reason for not doing something and an excuse. A reason explains how a conclusion is reached. An excuse explains why nothing was done about the conclusion. A reason is usually sincere. An excuse is generally a rationalization. A reason is real, whereas an excuse is at least an invention and at best a very weak reason. Christopher Smart characterized excuses more severely when he wrote, "An

Excuse is worse and more terrible than a Lie; for an Excuse is a Lie guarded."[7]

The Excuse of Lack of Ability

"I can't do that" is the most dangerous excuse, because you are often capable of more than you realize. For centuries, people of God have had to overcome this trap in order to excel.

When God called Moses to lead the Israelites out of Egypt, Moses answered, "Who am I that I should go to Pharaoh, and that I should bring the children of Israel out of Egypt?" (Ex. 3:11). Even after God had turned Moses's rod into a serpent, Moses continued to protest: "O my Lord, I am not eloquent ... but I am slow of speech and slow of tongue" (Ex. 4:10). Moses felt inferior. "My mouth gets dry," he said. "My tongue won't move; my knees knock. I can't be your message bearer."

I can sympathize with Moses. I have felt that way, too. Often when I've questioned my abilities, the Lord has said, "Go on ... keep going on, and I will be with you." That's certainly what He told Moses when He answered, "I will be with your mouth ... and I will teach you what you shall do" (Ex. 4:15).

People who have great talents are not usually the ones who get things done! Many would have rated John Beekman 4F for missionary service, and many would have considered D. L. Moody a failure because he only had a fifth-grade education. When he was a young man, Moody's theological knowledge was so limited that neither he nor the church he attended thought him qualified to teach Sunday school. Yet God used him to move two continents toward heaven.

Moody often said,

There are but few now that say, "Here am I, Lord; send me"; the cry now is, "Send some one else. Send the minister, send the church officers, the church wardens, the elders; but not me. I have not got the ability, the gifts, or the talents." Ah! honestly say you have not got the heart; for if the heart is loyal, God can use you. It is really all a matter of heart. It does not take God a great while to qualify a man for his work, if he only has the heart for it.[8]

When God wants to get a job done, He doesn't always look for a person with tremendous talents or great abilities. He looks for a person who is committed. He looks for someone who is willing to go anywhere, pay any price, and do His will.

The best way to get started is to get started! Don't mull over all the pros and cons of the job. Don't analyze and alibi. Start where you are and do what you can.

The Excuse of Being Too Busy

The second most common excuse is "I'm doing too much already. I'm too busy." There is a difference between busyness and really being busy. Some people look and sound busy, but they are merely disorganized. These people often excuse their own laziness by giving the name of "fanaticism" to the more ardent zeal of others.

Regardless of circumstances, we generally do what we want to do. Our feet follow our hearts. We use alibis, and sometimes we convince ourselves that we can't do what we ought to do.

We may say we don't feel well enough for our tasks and really believe we'll have more energy for them later.

Scripture is diametrically opposed to procrastination. It demands that we act now. Centuries ago at Shechem, Joshua demanded, "Choose for yourselves this day whom you will serve" (Josh. 24:15). He had a bias for action as did many other leaders in the Bible. Paul urged, "Now is the accepted time; behold, now is the day of salvation" (2 Cor. 6:2).

One of Jesus' best-known parables tells us what happens to those who do not act: "Everyone who hears these sayings of Mine, and does not do them, will be like a foolish man who built his house on the sand: and the rain descended, the floods came, and the winds blew and beat on that house; and it fell" (Matt. 7:26–27).

"Wait a minute," you might say, "you said in the last chapter that being is more important than doing." And it is. After all, it is possible to work yourself into a corpse and be a totally colorless person. But if someone has character, action should follow. Nothing worthwhile would get done if it didn't.

John Beekman's heart condition could have slowed him down to little or no action. He could have rationalized, "I'm doing too much. I need to rest." Instead he worked so hard that in 1955, the Chol New Testament was completed. John finally could not ignore the viselike pains in his chest. He and Elaine went to see the world-famous cardiologist Demetrio Sodi in Mexico City.

"You suffer from aortic insufficiency," said Dr. Sodi. "In simplest terms, this means some of your blood, after leaving your left ventricle, regurgitates and flows backward into your heart. This has caused your heart to work harder, which in turn has caused it to enlarge and subsequently cause your abnormally high blood pressure. It is a complete mystery to me how you ever walked those steep, rugged mountain trails in Chol country, because, in short, your heart is in congestive failure." . . .

John also learned from Dr. Sodi that a Dr. Charles Hufnagel of Georgetown University Hospital in Washington, D.C. had developed a plastic valve for aortic problems.

Dr. Sodi said, "If you are willing to take a risk—and the risk is great—he might be able to help you with your problem."[9]

John and his wife soon learned that Sodi was right; the risk was great. Only four such operations had ever been performed. Two of the four patients had survived. But if the operation was successful, John could have five more years, provided his activity was restricted.

John opted for surgery, and the plastic valve was inserted, at first causing a dangerous flutter but finally leveling out to a constant beat. John Beekman became survivor number three.

A new beat formed a quiet background to John's life, the continual ticktock of the plastic ball in the valve rising and falling in rhythm to his heartbeat. It was a sound many people might think strange, but his wife considered it "the most wonderful sound she had ever heard. 'As long as I hear the ticking,' she said, 'I'll know he's alive!'"[10]

A friend once asked if John's heart operation changed his

attitude toward his work. John replied, "From the beginning of our work with the Chols, Elaine and I determined to follow through as quickly as possible on whatever task we started, and that determination has carried through to this very day. What changed with my heart operation was a sensitivity in choosing priorities."[11]

John Beekman decided to spend his remaining years as wisely as a man spending his last dollar. This decision prompted him to found a Bible college at a place he named Berea. He said, "I believe the best use of my time would be to have the Chol men come to me, rather than me try to go to them."[12]

Beekman also reserved time for his translation work. The directors of Wycliffe's Mexico branch asked him to help translators who were having problems. His consultation work so impressed the Wycliffe Board of Directors that they assigned him to the newly created post of International Translation Coordinator in 1961.

John arranged for qualified Greek professors to spend their sabbaticals or summer vacations lecturing at the language center he founded in Ixmiquilpan. He began a quarterly paper, *Notes of Translation*, which was sent to all Wycliffe personnel. He later enlisted the new computer technology to develop an index to a Greek lexicon arranged by book, chapter, and verse for easy reference.[13]

Years of dedicated work stretched on for five years beyond the five Hufnagel had given him to live. Then ten. In 1971, John Beekman contracted malaria while he was conducting a workshop in Ghana, West Africa. He tried to fight the disease by taking aspirin, which would not aggravate his heart condition, but the high fevers, chills, and crushing headaches would not respond.

So he took the prescribed medicine, which had a quinine base. The next day his heart began to throb out of time, then miss beats. John had to leave Ghana for his home in New Jersey, and he finally returned to Mexico City to Dr. Sodi, who hospitalized him and supervised a series of potassium treatments. Miraculously, John's heart began to beat properly again.

Of course, he continued his work in Mexico. Only when the Wycliffe organization entreated him to join the staff of their new International Linguistic Center near Dallas was he convinced to leave his adopted land. For two years he lectured to Bible translators, worked on translation helps, and polished his book *Translating the Word of God.*

In February 1973, almost twenty years after his first heart surgery, John's angina pains became so severe that Dr. Michael DeBakery of Houston's Methodist Hospital recommended another operation. The Hufnagel valve had only recycled some of the blood regurgitating back into his heart. A second valve, placed right in the heart, would correct the erratic heartbeats that caused John such pain.[14]

Again the operation was successful, even though John hemorrhaged after the procedure and had to be rushed back into surgery. He returned to his work at the center and was able to return to Chiapas for a nostalgic visit in 1977. There he found more than twelve thousand Christians![15]

In the next year, John Beekman was advised again and again to retire. "I don't listen to that kind of advice," he always replied. "As long as I'm here, I want to use whatever strength I have to be of some service in His work."[16]

Beekman died in 1980, at the age of sixty-one. No one had expected him to live long, but he had. He was supposed to take it easy, but he didn't. Instead, his work led to the conversion of thousands of Chol Indians and the translation of the Bible into many languages all over the world. John Beekman was a man of action—careful, deliberate, dedicated, relentless action. He was one of the leading Bible translators of the twentieth century. He was a man committed to excellence.

You, like John Beekman, can experience excellence as you—right now—allow God to live His life in you and through you. First, you must translate your desire to please God into a commitment strong enough to last a lifetime. Then you must act; you must be willing to experiment, to fail at times in order to succeed. And throughout your journey through life, you must beware of the pitfalls of excuse making.

God uses ordinary people to accomplish miracles. Look at the lives of D. L. Moody, John Beekman, and many other great leaders. It may sound trivial, even simplistic, but a bias for action is a vital stepping-stone in the pursuit of excellence. So, my friend, get ready, get set, and by all means . . . GO!

Better say, "This one thing I do," than to say, "These fifty things I dabble in."

D. L. Moody

If you don't have a goal, any road will get you there.

Attributed to Yogi Berra, New York Yankees catcher

Only a mediocre person is always at his best.

Attributed to W. Somerset Maughan

5

SINGLE-MINDEDNESS —FOR A LIFETIME

"I will give them singleness of heart and action,
so that they will always fear me and that all will then
go well for them and for their children after them."

Jeremiah 32:39 NIV

One thing I ask from the LORD, this only do I seek:
that I may dwell in the house of the LORD all
the days of my life, to gaze on the beauty
of the LORD and to seek him in his temple.

Psalm 27:4 NIV

"The light of the body is the eye: if therefore
thine eye be single, thy whole body shall be full of light."

Matthew 6:22 KJV

I was the proud owner of an attractive jackknife when I was a boy. The knife had three blades, plus a can opener, a gimlet, a corkscrew, a nail file, and a miniature pair of scissors. The whole thing cost only a dollar, but wasn't worth a dime. The knife was so versatile that it was ineffective. None of the individual parts worked well enough to stand alone. Versatility can be a plus, but frequently it results in a lack of depth.

The same principle follows in our own lives. A versatile

person is all too often the man John Dryden described in one of his poems:

> A man so various, that he seem'd to be
> Not one, but all Mankind's Epitome:
> Stiff in opinions, always in the wrong;
> Was everything by starts, and nothing long;
> But in the course of one revolving moon,
> Was chemist, fiddler, statesman, and buffoon.[1]

STICK TO THE KNITTING

Peters and Waterman tell us that excellent companies have a tendency to focus on a few key business values and objectives, which enables them to keep everyone concentrating on the same top priorities. They call this tendency "Stick to the Knitting." The authors vigorously criticize the "merger mania" of the 1950s and 1960s. They laud corporate officials like Robert Wood Johnson, founder of Johnson and Johnson, who advised his successor, "Never acquire any business that you don't know how to run."[2] They suggest that excellent companies maintain the perspective of Procter and Gamble's former president Edward Harness, who said, "This company has never left its base. We seek to be anything but a conglomerate."[3]

Obviously some companies have diversified successfully, but most of them have kept close to their original expertise. The same principle is applicable to each of us. Jesus encouraged His hearers to have a single vision: "The light of the body is the eye: if therefore thine eye be single, thy whole body shall be full of light" (Matt. 6:22 KJV).

Jesus seemed to say, "Be a one-eyed person. Learn to do common things uncommonly well." Once we know who we are as children of God and desire to serve Him, we are ready to establish our lifetime goals—and then stick to them. Single-mindedness is required in the pursuit of excellence.

SET LIFETIME GOALS

I set my lifetime goals when I was only fourteen. That year, my parents moved our entire family to a new, dynamic church that catered to the young and challenged them to world evangelization. Each summer, from July 1 through Labor Day, special guests were invited to preach—noted ministers such as A. W. Tozer, Martin Lloyd-Jones, Samuel Zwemer, Martin DeHaan, and Billy Graham.

On the night of August 16, 1940, the guest speaker was David Otis Fuller. His message centered on being real: a dynamic faith versus a false faith. Although I was familiar with the teachings of the Bible, I had neglected to obey the truths I claimed to believe. Like Joseph of Arimathea, I was silent about my faith in Christ.

The main emphasis of Fuller's challenge was a verse from James, which grabbed me with such force that I could never be the same again: "Be doers of the word, and not hearers only, deceiving yourselves" (James 1:22).

That evening I barely noticed the ten-mile bus ride and the three-mile walk to my home as I prayed and thought about my future. My mother, who never went to bed until all her children were home, was awake when I got back to the house. I shared my experience with her, and she intuitively understood that something significant and life-changing had taken place in my life.

"Your father and I dedicated you to the Lord before you were born," she told me. "If God calls you to preach, don't shrink and become anything else." She warmly told me about God's love in her own life and then committed me to God's care.

My bedroom was a small, unheated area, which had once been an attic. That night as I knelt alone in my room, I wrote down my first goals in life. Although I was an average teenager, I formed four goals that have grown and intensified throughout the passing years.

Seek, above everything else, to bring glory to God
(see 1 Cor. 10:31).
Cultivate the inner life (see 2 Peter 3:18).
Disciple as many people as humanly possible
(see Matt. 28:19–20).
Win as many people to Jesus Christ as possible
(see Prov. 11:30).

Once goals like these are set, the struggle is to fulfill them single-mindedly. Single-mindedness does not come pre-wrapped and ready to go. It must be cultivated, encouraged, and seriously undertaken. I have a sign on my desk that reads: "Keep off the detours." At times in my life, I mentally have had to yank myself off a detour and back onto the main street.

I learned long ago that even good things can rob me of that which is best.

RECOGNIZE THE DETOURS

When I began public ministry, I combined preaching with my artistic talent. I illustrated the theme of my message on a large, nine-foot easel.

This easel was illuminated by colored lights, and I often drew with fluorescent chalk.

Sometimes I drew a picture of the Holy City and the glory of the life that awaits us. In the foreground I sketched the apostle John standing on the Island of Patmos and gazing into the distance. Then I quickly drew in the outline of the Holy City in fluorescent yellows, oranges, and whites and surrounded this with white rays to convey brilliance. I knew this technique was effective. Once while I was drawing this picture for an audience in Chicago, a soldier recently returned from Vietnam came to me before I had finished and said, "Help me get ready for heaven."

In New Hampshire, while I was drawing another picture, the "Haven of Rest," an elderly woman bowed her head and asked the Lord to be her Savior. I have met literally thousands of men and women who could remember a picture I had drawn many years earlier and who could explain clearly its message.

I had always known, however, that my primary call was to be a pastor, teacher, and evangelist. I began to realize that the artistic illustrations took a great deal of time from the actual message, and in a way they became a crutch. They also limited the number of people I could reach at one time; far more people could hear a message than could see those pictures, even if I enlarged my drawing surface to eight feet.

I felt a deep, inner conviction to devote all my efforts to preaching, a longing that I sensed as God's direction, no matter how traumatic it would be for me. If God was for it, who could be against it? I purposed in my heart to be single-minded, to allow nothing to deflect the magnetic needle of my calling. God honored that decision by sharpening my speaking gift and providing more invitations than I could ever accept. I had learned to get off the detours and onto the main road, which required constant reappraisal of my goals in life and an evaluation of whether or not they were being accomplished.

ASK THE PROPER QUESTIONS

We must ask ourselves specific questions to evaluate what we are doing. The first question should align us with the proper motive: "Is what I am doing really serving God, or is it serving my pride, my selfishness, or even the devil?" After all, Jesus told us, "No servant can serve two masters; for either he will hate the one and love the other, or else he will be loyal to the one and despise the other. You cannot serve God and mammon" (Luke 16:13).

"Where am I going?" should be the next question. Twice a year, on New Year's Day and on July 1, I take a personal inventory. I write a list of specific goals for the next six months in the following order: spiritual, intellectual, social, physical, and financial. I list goals such as "knowing God and His power" under the spiritual category, and "becoming a caring person" and "being the best husband and father possible" under the social category. I try to write one book a year, so completion of that year's book is usually one of my intellectual goals.

Then I list the steps I must take to reach those goals, a job that is nearly as important as writing out the goals in the first place. For instance, I set aside time each weekday morning for writing.

Every month I look at these goals and take inventory. Though I seldom realize all my goals, the results have been good. Goals keep me from running around like the proverbial chicken with its head cut off, not knowing where I am going. Following this method should help you realize your goals, too.

Throughout the year I have learned to delegate and supervise, instead of trying to do everything myself. I remind myself that biblical leaders like Moses had to learn this management technique. After Moses led the Israelites out of Egypt, he attempted to minister to the people personally. The Israelites waited from early morning until evening to tell Moses their problems and have him settle their disputes. You can imagine the lines and the confusion!

Moses's father-in-law, Jethro, could not understand this practice. He asked,

> Why do you alone sit. . . . Both you and these people who are with you will surely wear yourselves out. For this thing is too much for you. . . . Select from all the people able men, such as fear God, men of truth, hating covetousness; and place such over them . . . rulers of thousands, rulers of

hundreds, rulers of fifties, and rulers of tens. And let them judge the people at all times. (Ex. 18:14, 18, 21–22)

In essence, Jethro said, "Delegate, Moses, or you—and your people—will perish!"

Moses had sense enough to listen. Only the most difficult cases were brought before Moses himself, a good principle for everyone. We must delegate in order to be effective.

I have also learned to say "No." A kind, yet firm, no is vital to single-mindedness. When I became senior pastor of Chicago's Moody Church, I found myself inundated with speaking invitations. I decided to accept only one invitation each month.

WATCH OUT FOR DOUBLE-MINDEDNESS

One great barrier to single-mindedness is worry. Our English word *worry* is equivalent to the Greek words *merizo*, meaning "to divide," and *nous*, meaning "mind." Worry really means "to divide the mind." It means we are double-minded rather than single-minded. The apostle James warned, "A double-minded man [is] unstable in all his ways" (James 1:8).

When we are double-minded, we resemble a monster with two heads facing opposite directions, or we are like a rudderless boat, unable to steer straight, "driven and tossed by the wind" (James 1:6).

Charles Haddon Spurgeon, a great nineteenth-century preacher, once said that he worried for weeks before a speaking engagement, even to the extent of hoping he would break a leg and miss the event. When he finally entered the pulpit to give the speech, he was exhausted.

Then Spurgeon faced up to his fear. He asked himself, What is the worst thing that could happen to me during my sermon? Whatever it was, he decided, the heavens would not collapse. He knew that he had been magnifying his fears. Once he faced his worries for what they were, he relaxed, simply because his mind was no longer divided. His single-mindedness led him to excel at preaching, the ministry he once feared most.

There is no sight sublime, no influence so resistless, no nobility so Godlike as that of a man or woman doing one thing right for the glory of God. Unfortunately, too many of us change our goals so often that progress is impossible. Single-mindedness for a lifetime is a MUST!

The pastor of my boyhood church served the same church for over sixty years. Think of that—sixty years! Instead of switching from church to church, he wisely enlarged the outreach of his ministry in the place God put him. He was a choice role model to me and to hundreds of others.

The Reverend Herrmann George Braunlin first went to Hawthorne, New Jersey, to be the song leader for a small Bible study group that formed after a citywide Billy Sunday evangelistic campaign in 1924. At the time, he was a bookkeeper for a New York silk firm.

Braunlin never attended college or seminary; he simply devoured countless books and mastered the English Bible. Under his leadership, the Bible study group became a mission and then a small church body.

In the first twenty years of his ministry, he began three

outreaches. The first, a daily radio program called *Inspiration Time*, began in the 1940s. Originally aired over WPAT, and heard in northern New Jersey and New York City.

The second outreach was the Hawthorne Evening Bible School, developed from the Sunday school teacher training program many churches conduct. Braunlin perceived the layman's lack of spiritual knowledge and a hunger for good teaching, so he developed a program that extended beyond a short time frame and beyond the limited goals of preparing teachers to lead specific classes. Soon, hundreds of people in the area were attending a Monday evening Bible school taught by gifted local pastors. Some of these students gave themselves to years of full-time ministry.

A third outreach was a summer Bible conference, which continued for over fifty years. However, as the local church grew in size, specific ministries were created to meet the needs of a dynamic congregation all year long, and the summer conference was discontinued.

Today the church faithfully and effectively seeks to evangelize the entire metropolitan area.

October 5, 1995, Hermann G. Braunlin was promoted into the presence of God. He served the Lord and the Lord's people with a single mind, to the glory of God.

When I personally have faced difficult decisions throughout the years, I have invariably asked myself, "How would Pastor Braunlin handle this situation?" For one thing, he never shot from the hip. I never saw him lose his temper. Lovingly, patiently, fairly—yet firmly—he faced conflicts with the single goal of glorifying God.

Without his single-minded dedication, the Hawthorne Gospel Church might never have excelled.

That small Bible study group, formed after the Billy Sunday crusade, conceivably might have slowly dissolved as its members became preoccupied with the concerns of their families and everyday life. Single-mindedness is without doubt one of the attributes God uses to accomplish His work here on earth. Single-mindedness is a mark of excellence.

God calls us all to evaluate the talents He has given us. We need to set lifetime goals and then pursue them single-mindedly, while continually avoiding the distractions—good and bad—that would pull us in many different directions.

Dr. Charles Ryrie once reminded me, "The main thing in life is to keep the main thing the main thing." I believe he was calling for single-mindedness for a lifetime!

. . . these three remain: faith, hope and love. But the greatest of these is love.

1 Corinthians 13:13 NIV

Where [love] is wanting, the beauty of all virtues is mere tinsel—is empty sound—is not worth a straw—nay more, is offensive and disgusting.

John Calvin

Keep yourselves in God's love as you wait for the mercy of our Lord Jesus Christ to bring you to eternal life.

Jude 21 NIV

6

LOVE—THE MENDER OF SOULS

... I will show you the most excellent way.

1 Corinthians 12:31 NIV

"By this everyone will know that you are
my disciples, if you love one another."

John 13:35 NIV

Love is the only spiritual power that can overcome the
self-centeredness that is inherent in being alive. Love
is the thing that makes life possible or, indeed, tolerable.

Arnold Toynbee

I can recall a time when the subject of God's love had little appeal to me. For various reasons, I thought of God's love as soft and sentimental—maybe impractical. I imagined that God's love was a convenient excuse for spineless Christians.

"We must accept him in love," some people would say, to avoid confronting a brother when he violated God's Word.

My Scottish-immigrant background also influenced my feelings. Mom and Dad were deeply caring people, whom I loved and greatly respected. However, neither of them were given to undue emotion. I cannot remember ever seeing my father cry. For the most part, he hid his feelings except for an occasional outbreak of impatience. My father claimed he had lost the ability to cry.

My mother, too, buried her feelings. She had experienced deep wounds, which began with her mother's death when Mom was only three. Her sorrow didn't ebb as she grew older. Instead, a stepmother who was less than fair increased her sadness and isolation. The home situation was so traumatic that her only sister, Annie, ran away at age twelve, never to be heard from again. I remember my mother's saying to us, during life's wrenching experiences, "We Scots don't wear our feelings on our sleeves." She was really saying, "We don't cry; we hide our tears."

As a child I was also crowned with a full head of curls, which only made it more difficult for me to defend myself against my peers. At times, when I needed an infusion of courage to face my tormentors, Mother would say, "Laddie, the blood of the Covenanters is in your veins." After those words, I was ready to take on the whole neighborhood. Yes, I must confess, to my shame, I was a scrapper. I somehow thought I had to be strong, so I saw little future in anything as submissive and gentle as love.

But serious sickness helps you focus on what really matters. The days in the hospital after my cancer surgery in 1944 were life-changing for me. I reread the biography of D. L. Moody and was moved by his commitment to God's love. "I got full of it," Moody said. "It ran out my fingers. *You* take up the subject of love *in the Bible*! You will get so full of it that all you have got to do is to open your lips, and a flood of the Love of God flows out."[1]

Slowly, I, too, experienced the transforming power of God's love. I remember the warm sense of worth and assurance as I prayed, "Lord, this hospital bed is my altar. I want to adjust my life to Your sovereign will. And Lord, if You don't mind . . . I'd like to be *a living* sacrifice. Amen."

Then I reached for a pad and wrote out another lifetime goal: I commit my life, from this moment forward, to be a channel of Your divine love. By the grace of God, I had come to realize my mistake and the pressing need to pursue God's love as an all-important mark of excellence.

However, many people today use the word *love* carelessly and incorrectly. Sometimes the word is used romantically. Other times it is used to describe lust. One television network advertises its afternoon of soap operas as "love in the afternoon." The word *love* is also employed to state a preference: "I just love butter pecan ice cream."

The so-called new morality has increased the confusion by stating that there are no absolutes in our world except love and that whatever is done in love must be right. Of course, I cannot accept that view. The only love that leads to excellence is God's love, which is holy, humble, honest, and faithful. True love is much tougher than I ever imagined. The apostle Paul made this clear. "Love suffers long," he said. Love bears. Love endures. Love hangs in there.

The love Paul described is not easy. It means staying with a husband or wife when things go wrong and that person doesn't seem to be the perfect spouse you thought you married. It means loving your enemies, not just those who are nice to you. Love is a day-by-day battle to put aside your desire to serve yourself, so you can serve God and your fellow human beings.

Some Christians fail to show such love. They have accepted Christ as their Savior, but they do not commit themselves to following the life He requires. This behavior is nothing new. Certainly the Pharisees did not show God's love even though this truth was taught in Old Testament times by Moses (see Deut. 6:5) and reaffirmed by Jesus when a lawyer asked Him, "Teacher, which is the great commandment in the law?"

Jesus answered, "'You shall love the LORD your God with all your heart, with all your soul, and with all your mind.' This is the first and great commandment" (Matt. 22:36–38).

LOVE GOD

Our love for God may seem weak at first, since we feel we don't really know Him, but our human relationships begin the same way. Other people's love for us makes us respond to them in friendship and love. The principle is the same in the spiritual realm. We love God because He first loved us (see 1 John 4:9). Think of the power of the love of an omnipotent God—a love so great we could never deserve it! God only asks that we love Him in return.

George Verwer, a dynamic missionary-evangelist whose goal is to live a life of love, says true love begins with a hunger for God, which is a genuine mark of the disciple. He states, "If you yearn for deep fellowship with your Creator, if you desire to know him intimately and to walk with him and to breathe with him—though you may look like a failure and have made innumerable blunders, then you are well on the road to discipleship."[2]

LOVE YOUR NEIGHBOR

Jesus gave the lawyer a second commandment: "You shall love your neighbor as yourself" (Matt. 22:39). The Pharisees were devastated by His words. Jesus was saying that unless they loved God and others fully, all their good deeds and sacrifices were wasted efforts. These misguided men knew how to wash their hands just to keep from being ceremonially unclean, but loving their neighbors—that was too much to ask! Similarly, Paul told the Christians at Corinth: "Now abide faith, hope, love, these three; but the greatest of these is love" (1 Cor. 13:13).

Jesus and Paul were both requiring a new mark to identify Christians, not the crosses many wear today, not the emblem of a fish, an ox's yoke, or a shepherd's staff. Jesus identified this mark so there would be no confusion: "By this all will know that you are My disciples, if you have love for one another" (John 13:35). Without this mark, "I am nothing" (1 Cor. 13:2), and "it profits me nothing" (1 Cor. 13:3). Is there anything less than nothing?

The apostle Paul went on to challenge the Corinthians to make God's love their goal. "Follow after love" (1 Cor. 14:1 ASV), he said. The word *follow* is a strenuous word. The same Greek word is used to describe Paul's fierce pursuit and persecution of the early Christians prior to his conversion. It is the same word Paul used when he spoke of pressing "toward the goal for the prize of the upward call of God in Christ Jesus" (Phil. 3:14).

At times my commitment to live out God's love has faltered, and I have given in to my natural desire for ease and material possessions. At those moments, I have had to take the flesh hooks, as did the priests in the Old Testament, and sink them into my life, adjusting myself to the center of God's altar.

I remember one time when I was speaking at a church in Michigan. At the end of the service, I was painfully aware that I had failed. There seemed to be little explanation for it, but little had gone right. After the people left the church, I stayed and knelt at the front pew. I prayed. I wept. My heart was broken before God. The Lord made me painfully aware of my dishonest self and of my own personal, selfish ambitions. I enjoyed the thrill of speaking to large audiences. Enjoyed their approval and commendations. Rather than being a voice for God, I was really representing myself. I told the Lord that I needed help—His help—right away.

That morning, as I poured out my soul in confession, I made up my mind to pray daily for the gift of love. I translated a lifetime goal into a daily commitment, which is necessary for excellence. I asked the Lord to help me follow after love, to make the love of God the very center of my entire life. The difference since that day has been life-changing. God's love has become my dynamic purpose. Today, more than ever before, I am convinced that this love shining through me and through others, working through us, is the answer to the conflicts of our lost world.

George Verwer sees Christianity as a "revolution of love."

> I asked the Lord to help me follow after love, to make the love of God the very center of my entire life.

Why? Because any individual who would live the life Jesus preached is of "necessity a revolutionary individual, a cultural nonconformist, a 'fanatic,' if you please!" Verwer says, "Literal adherence to the principle laid down by Jesus would, without a doubt, result in a worldwide revolution—a revolution motivated by love, a revolution executed by love, and a revolution culminating in love!"[3]

PRACTICE LOVE

Francis Schaeffer wrote, "Upon His authority, He gives the world the right to judge whether you and I are born-again Christians on the basis of our observable love toward all Christians."[4] This is a sobering and wondrous fact. The world has the right to judge the reality of our profession of faith on the basis of the love we show each other. Even more important, the world can use this mark to judge whether or not Jesus is the Son of God. Imagine! Our lack of love for each other can deny the belief we hold most dear.

Unfortunately, loving our neighbors often seems more like a lofty ideal than a practical reality that we show each day of our lives. Love is caring for others as we care for ourselves, day in and day out. George Verwer suggests,

Perhaps we can understand love better if we use the word "care." You have been caring for yourself all day long, ever since this morning when you woke up and your self-love automatically went right into action. . . . Shortly after getting out of bed, you had a little pain in your tummy—very slight, but enough to get you into action. Immediately you started toward the coffeepot and bread and jam.[5]

This is love in action, a reality that feeds the hungry and helps those who hurt.

Well, how do you rate? How do your neighbors and fellow workers perceive you? As someone who listens when they have problems? What about your own family? Is there a relative you dislike—or even hate? A sister or brother-in-law whom you resent? If so, you had better heed the apostle John's warning:

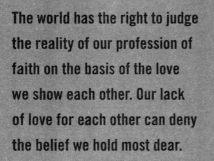

The world has the right to judge the reality of our profession of faith on the basis of the love we show each other. Our lack of love for each other can deny the belief we hold most dear.

"If someone says, 'I love God,' and hates his brother, he is a liar; for he who does not love his brother whom he has seen, how can he love God whom he has not seen?" (1 John 4:20). Be your own judge. Do you truly love God?

"But what can I do in situation where bitterness and anger have prevailed?" you reply. "It is impossible for me to love my mother-in-law or the person in the church who is constantly criticizing me." It is true that some people are more difficult to love than others. What you must do is *love by faith*. Faith is the starting place.

I counseled a woman in her midtwenties whose story was one of failure, rebellion, and bitterness toward her parents, which had led to a lack of communication with her family for more than four years. Silence turned to anger and then to hatred.

As I shared the possibility of God's love with her, she was visibly moved to repentance and faith in Jesus Christ. After praying the sinner's prayer, she looked up and whispered, "Now I must go home and make things right with my family, but how can I love after all my bitter words?"

My answer was, "You must begin to love by faith." I encouraged her to ask God to give her the spirit that forgives and forgets. Just as she had exercised faith to receive Christ as her Savior, so she needed faith to love and be reconciled to her parents. That day, the young woman began a journey of love by faith that eventually led to the uniting of an entire family.

Often I've had to love by faith. My approach is to begin by sincerely praying for the person I'm having the conflict with. I ask God specifically to resolve the situation. Remember, only when Job prayed for his miserable comforters was he released from his own captivity. "And the LORD turned the captivity of Job, when he prayed for his friends" (Job 42:10 KJV).

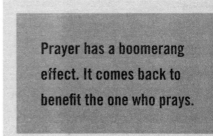

Prayer has a boomerang effect. It comes back to benefit the one who prays.

Prayer has a boomerang effect. It comes back to benefit the one who prays. Praying for a troubling relationship in your life will help you both. Perhaps you will want to make a list of the person's good qualities and even the bad ones. Then, in an act of genuine faith, resolve to love that person. I have seen thousands of people learn to love by faith.

A REVOLUTION OF LOVE

I have mentioned George Verwer's commitment to a revolution of love. You may be wondering if this is all talk or if Verwer really has begun such a revolution. His story will provide some answers for you.

Soon after he graduated from Moody Bible Institute, Verwer led a group of students to evangelize Mexico. In a short time, Christian bookstores were opened and Christian radio broadcasts begun, even though they had been forbidden by the government.

This faith adventure led the students to intercede for Spain, a country formerly closed to most mission endeavors. By 1961, Verwer and his small band of students dedicated themselves to a world revolution of love:

> We are only a small group of Christian young people in Operation Mobilization, yet we have determined by God's grace to live our lives according to the revolutionary teaching of our Master. . . . Every petty, personal desire must be subordinated to the supreme task of reaching the world for Christ. . . . We must be ready to suffer for him and count it joy, to die for him and count it gain. . . . This is our commitment, and we will press forward until every person has heard the gospel.[6]

In 1962, two hundred young people from thirty nations went to Western Europe to distribute Bibles and other Christian literature and to confront people with the message of salvation. Each new development was initiated and sustained in faith-exercising prayer, and all over Europe, teams worked with local churches and helped them reach their own communities more effectively. Fourteen new churches resulted from their efforts in France alone.

During an extended time of prayer in 1964, God gave Verwer and his young people a creative idea. To reach people for Christ, they could use a ship to sail the oceans of the world and dock at ports on different continents. Their prayer was answered: donations enabled them to buy a large oceangoing vessel, and sailing crews from several countries offered their services without salary. People from every continent have visited the ship, the *Logos*, and untold numbers have received Christ. A second ship, the *Doulos*, was added in 1971. In 1988, *Logos II* replaced the *Logos*, which had run aground, suffering irreparable damage.

Why is Operation Mobilization so effective? Listen to George Verwer describe just one day in this revolution of love:

> We will never forget a one-day campaign we had in Bombay some months ago, when the Lord had laid it on our hearts to distribute a half million tracts in one day. After having distributed some 400,000 tracts throughout the day, we had a meeting in the evening. As we closed that meeting we said that if anyone was constrained to go back into the streets with tracts, we still had a few left . . . about 100,000! There were several volunteers. I had absolutely no desire to go out that night with more tracts.
>
> It was 11 p.m., we had started the day at 5 a.m., and I had worked through the night before on the maps of the

city. I was tired. I did not feel any love tingling through me. And as I started out. . . . I saw Him going the second mile—I saw Him going up Calvary's hill for me. **That was love!** It was not cheap sentiment. . . . It was **action.** And I said to myself that if Jesus could go the extra mile for me, then surely He could help me go the extra mile for those others whom He loved. . . .

We went out into the streets of Bombay again, and around midnight I could see for about a quarter of a mile in front of us around five thousand men and women sleeping on the pavement. I've never before seen such a sight in my life. I had two big bags filled with tracts and for the first time in my life, I went from "bed to bed," giving out tracts!

This world in which we live is a sick world. It is a world of misery and tragedy such as most of us cannot begin to imagine. Millions are sleeping on pavements, starving to death, knowing nothing of the love of God for them. The church sings, "My Jesus, I love Thee." And at the same time **150,000 people a day slip away into eternity.** And we say that we love them. I say we don't. If we loved them with Christ's love, we wouldn't stop until we had sold a million books and distributed 100 million tracts. And as we did it, our tears could bathe these lost souls. I know too little about it. I have wept little over souls and much over my unloving heart. But I can say before God, "**I WANT IT!**" You can take all that I have! You can take my family (and I do not say this lightly), **BUT I WANT A LIFE OF LOVE! I WANT GOD!**[7]

But what about today?

That once small band of students now numbers more than three thousand serving in O.M., with another fourteen hundred serving as interns, volunteers, associates, and second workers in their training programs.

Lawrence Tong, International Director, wrote in his 2016 annual report, "We have a presence today in over 110 nations, plus many others served by the O.M. ships."

Tong says, "Our tactics are diverse, but our commitment to the Great Commission has never wavered."[8]

Yes, Verwer's love had sparked a revolution. George Verwer is a man committed to the pursuit of excellence. How about your love for God? Has it made a difference to you? To your neighbors? To your world?

Little in life is permanent. Everything in this life fails. Jobs fail. Health fails. Fame fails. Wealth fails. Only "love never fails" (1 Cor. 13:8). If you are consumed with God's love, if you share His love with others, if you practice it each day, you too can start a revolution of love in your own home—in your own church—in your own neighborhood. Why not begin today?

Love is the excellent way. Of all the marks of excellence, love most forcefully proves God's existence and the reality of our faith in Him. Without love, we are nothing. A helpful equation to remember is: Life minus love . . . equals zero!

I owe more to the fire, and the hammer, and the file, than anything else in the Lord's workshop.

Charles Haddon Spurgeon (1834–1892)

The cross of Christ is the proof of God's . . . loving solidarity with us in our pain. . . . The God who allows us to suffer, once suffered himself in Christ, and continues to suffer with us and for us today.

John R. Stott, *The Cross of Christ*

SUFFERING—
THE REFINER'S FIRE

We are hard pressed on every side, but not crushed;
perplexed, but not in despair; persecuted, but
not abandoned; struck down, but not destroyed.

2 Corinthians 4:8–9 NIV

And the God of all grace, who called you to his
eternal glory in Christ, after you have suffered a
little while, will himself restore you and make
you strong, firm and steadfast.

1 Peter 5:10 NIV

If God exempted Christians from suffering, pastors could stop preaching, TV preachers could cancel their shows, and believers could stop witnessing. Nonbelievers would still throng to the church and wear out the carpeted aisles to the altar, for Christianity would be the modern-day panacea, a gold-plated insurance policy for happiness.

However, that's not God's plan. No conversion decision will ever shield a person from suffering, though some individuals seem to accept Christ on the basis of false theology, which they base on such promises as "Beloved, I pray that you may prosper in all things and be in health, just as your soul

> God doesn't promise us a rose garden. But He does promise to help us live in the brown, dried-out pasture in which we sometimes find ourselves.

prospers" (3 John 2). These new believers are either soon disillusioned or grow into an understanding that God doesn't promise us a rose garden. But He does promise to help us live in the brown, dried-out pasture in which we sometimes find ourselves.

Each of us responds to suffering with the natural question, Why? Why me, God? Men and women throughout the Bible struggled with this same question. Their answer is also our answer.

Gideon, whose story is told in the book of Judges, is an example of necessary suffering. God allowed the Midianites, fierce nomads who lived east of the Jordan River and down into the Sinai Peninsula, to conquer His people because the Hebrews had worshiped false gods. Gideon had to thresh grain secretly in his father's winepress, a large square pit in the ground, because the Midianites would swoop down and raid the camp as soon as they saw the telltale dust of threshing.

As Gideon was threshing, a stranger suddenly accosted him and said, "The LORD is with you, you mighty man of valor!" (Judg. 6:12). Gideon's response was much like ours might have been: "It doesn't look as if the Lord is with me! Here I am secretly beating out a harvest single-handedly. Our whole nation is hungry and suffering. Not one threshing floor is in operation. The Midianites have practically wiped us out.

And what's more, their false worship has invaded our land."

Why God? Why all the trouble? Many things in life make us ask why. A husband or wife may have left the family for a sexual relationship with another person, or a teenager may have become hopelessly hooked on drugs. We've all felt the panic and depression, the sick feeling in our stomachs, and the constant fear that we may not be able to withstand the pressure.

It is interesting that the little instrument used in Gideon's day to beat the grain and divide the chaff from the wheat was called a "tribulum." The English word *tribulation* comes from this word. Tribulation separates the chaff from the wheat in our lives; it often eliminates our selfish desires and allows our Godlike nature to grow.

> **Sometimes suffering is God's way of bringing us back to Him.**

Christians have frequently associated suffering with punishment. Suffering can be a consequence from sin, just as the Midianites victory over the Israelites was because the Israelites had begun to worship other gods. Sometimes suffering is God's way of bringing us back to Him.

SUFFERING OFTEN CHASTENS

Let's see what God had in mind for Gideon. God's answer to Gideon's *Why?* was, "Go in this might of yours, and you shall save Israel from the hand of Midianites. Have I not sent you?" (Judg. 6:14). God said, "Gideon, you have been chosen to change the situation."

Gideon looked at the condition of his father's house. He looked at the hordes of invading Midianites, but the Lord said, "You're looking in the wrong direction. Look at Me! Don't worry about the circumstances. I will deliver you." God knows that suffering always calls for faith—and lots of it.

Gideon, like Moses before him and thousands of Christians after him, was overcome by the task. *Who, me?* he thought. Our situation is impossible; I can't change it. He said, "O my Lord, how can I save Israel? Indeed my clan is the weakest in Manasseh, and I am the least in my father's house" (Judg. 6:15). But God's answer to Gideon's second *Why?* was simply a command to action. It was an order to get going, to get on with the job. And soon Gideon's army defeated the Midianite enemy!

Revelation 3:19 reads, "As many as I love, I rebuke and chasten." God would be a poor father if Christians were not chastened. The child who grows up to hold high standards of excellence in his or her life is rarely the one who received no discipline in the home. God holds us accountable for our actions.

A father who leaves his family for an affair will suffer the consequences. His children may become rebellious, questioning the beliefs he has taught them because of his infidelity to his wife. He may be led to overindulge in other sins, such as alcoholism or drug addiction. But sometimes this suffering leads him to God, just as it led the Israelites.

Suffering resulted from human rebellion against God. Adam's action in the garden of Eden opened the way for all of us to experience pain, distress, physical suffering, and spiritual questioning. But we must be careful to remember that not all suffering results from specific sin. We can't know or speculate why a person suffers any more than we can understand many of God's mysteries. Neither can we understand why God sometimes delivers one person from suffering and allows another person's suffering to continue.

> **We can't know or speculate why a person suffers any more than we can understand many of God's mysteries.**

SUFFERING FASHIONS OUR CHARACTER

Another explanation of suffering is that it often leads us to grow more like Jesus, the ultimate example of excellence. God wants us to be like Him, but becoming Godlike usually means pruning and cutting, pressure and pain. I can sincerely say that I learned more in six months of physical suffering than in years of health.

Many suffering people read the book of Job to find help because the entire book describes the suffering of one individual. Satan told God that Job seemed to have no problems. "Have You not made a hedge around him, around his household, and around all that he has on every side?" (Job 1:10). In essence, Satan said, "Job loves You because You have given him everything. He has never suffered." Job's love for God had never withstood a time of suffering, which is the real test of devotion.

Satan challenged God, "Stretch out Your hand and touch all that he has, and he will surely curse You to Your face!" (Job 1:11).

God answered, "All that he has is in your power; only do not lay a hand on his person" (Job 1:12). Notice that God did not cause Job's suffering—nor does He cause ours. However, He does allow Satan to test us.

In a few moments all Job's possessions were destroyed: his livestock, his servants, and his children!

What was Job's response? "Naked I came from my mother's womb, and naked shall I return there. The LORD gave, and the LORD has taken away; blessed be the name of the LORD" (Job 1:21). Job survived the first test and still gave the Lord his total trust.

Job realized that his possessions were gifts from God only loaned to him for a time.

So Satan tried again. He challenged God, "Stretch out Your hand now, and touch his bone and his flesh, and he will surely curse You to Your face!" (Job 2:5). Satan destroyed Job's possessions, and he wanted to destroy his physical body. But God restricted Satan's power; he was not allowed to kill Job.

Initially, Job's response to his physical suffering was not too different from what ours might be. He longed for death to take him out of his misery. He could not sleep because of his dreams and visions. He cried out, "My eye will never again see good" (Job 7:7), which is exactly what we think when we say we will never be happy again.

Job admitted, "For the thing I greatly feared has come upon me" (Job 3:25). How true it is that we are often tested in the area we worry most about. After all, such tests are the most meaningful to

> **We are often tested in the area we worry most about.**

us. If we worry about our health, we may face some dreaded disease or surgery. The false gods we tend to worship will fall.

Yet, in the midst of his many days of agony, Job declared, "I know that my Redeemer lives, and He shall stand at last on the earth; and after my skin is destroyed, this I know, that in my flesh I shall see God" (Job 19:25–26).

Job became a more confident believer in the midst of his suffering. What happened to him? The Lord blessed him more abundantly than he had been blessed the early days of his life. He had more possessions than before, and his health was so restored that he lived for 140 more years.

Remember that great roll call of heroes in Hebrews 11, the men and women who had such great faith. However, some in Hebrews 11 suffered even though they had "a good testimony through faith" (Heb. 11:36–39).

At God's request, Abraham left his family and friends and Haran to head out into the arid desert, where he faithfully followed God to Canaan. Joseph was attacked by his brothers, taken as a slave to Egypt, and later thrown into prison for a crime he didn't commit. God used the suffering of some, so they could experience even greater things, for God's glory.

Mr. R. DeHaan, a well-known radio Bible teacher of the 1950s, illustrated the refining process of suffering in this way:

An ordinary bar of steel is worth $5.00, but it doubles in value when the same bar is made into horseshoes. If transformed into needles, the bar is worth $350. But when hammered into springs for expensive watches, the same bar is worth $250,000. The pounding, heating, and cutting process required for springs increases the steel's value tremendously.[1] God allows us to be hammered and heated because He sees our ultimate worth. He sees through the cloudy rock to the sparkling diamond beneath.

DeHaan went on to observe that the most cheerful people are often the ones who have had the "least sunshine and the most pain and suffering in their lives. The most grateful people I have met were not those who had traveled a pathway of roses all their lives through, but those who were confined . . . to their homes—often to their beds. . . . The 'gripers,' on the other hand, are usually those who enjoy excellent health. The complainers are those who have the least to complain about."[2]

Margaret Clarkson, author and poet, wrote, "Many a sick, weakly soul cowers within a healthy body, while many a hopeless sufferer is perfectly whole in heart. . . . A healthy soul is a greater gift than a healthy body and this is something that none of us need lack."[3]

Yes, suffering often fashions our characters. Suffering allows the spirit of God within us to mold our flawed human nature back into His perfect image.

SUFFERING CAN GLORIFY GOD

The apostle Paul wrote, "I take pleasure in infirmities, in reproaches, in needs, in persecutions, in distresses, for Christ's sake. For when I am weak, then I am strong" (2 Cor. 12:10). That's a strange statement by the world's standards. Most of us refuse to accept weakness. We think pain should be avoided at all cost. Pain should be eradicated, medicated, or banished. Some individuals wander from doctor to doctor, church to church, drug to drug, seeking some means to dispel what they think is destroying the quality of their lives. Suffering is not the world's way. Society's idols are not the weak but the strong—the star quarterback, the powerful politician, the young corporate president.

When Christians question their suffering, writer Edith Schaeffer reminds them of 2 Corinthians 4:7: "We have this treasure in earthen vessels, that the excellence of the power may be of God and not of us." She said, "As I read that, I see cracked teapots, still usable despite a chip in the spout, a crack in the lid, or a wobbly handle, and still lovingly used by the one who knows its history."[4]

Christian excellence means suffering with and for Christ. Charles Haddon Spurgeon once said, "The Lord gets his best soldiers out of the highlands of affliction."

Many of us have had friends whose quiet patience and endurance of terminal illness—their constant ability to get up and start again after each setback—testified to God's power in their lives. One middle-aged woman left a Chicago hospital for a couple of hours to attend church only five days after brain surgery for a malignant tumor. A less motivated member of her congregation commented, "It's her faith that keeps her going. I may not agree with her born-again fervor, but I sure know that her courage comes from God. Her face shines with God's presence."

I know something of the battle a cancer patient wages. I know firsthand what it is like to hear the words, "It's malignant." In 1984, I experienced a second bout with cancer. A routine transurethral resection of the prostate revealed malignant chips requiring further radiation therapy.

Material things are empty in moments of weakness. Once again I understood the folly of possessions and the hope and assurance found in Jesus. My faith was anchored in the Lord. Ultimately, I knew that only that which is eternal . . . really matters!

I learned to see suffering as Paul saw it. In his second letter to the Corinthians, he told them, "When we came to Macedonia, our bodies had no rest, but we were troubled on every side. Outside were conflicts, inside were fears" (7:5). All of us know that Paul's fears were justified, yet he said,

> Our light affliction, which is but for a moment, is working for us a far more exceeding and eternal weight of glory, while we do not look at the things which are seen, but at the things which are not seen. For the things which are seen are temporary, but the things which are not seen are eternal. (2 Cor. 4:17–18)

God can use our suffering to reveal His greatness and He can use our suffering to accomplish His work here on earth.

SUFFERING BLESSES

Many heroes of modern Christianity, such as Moody, Spurgeon, and Carey, found that God used their suffering to their greatest achievements. I will tell their stories in chapters 11, 12, and 13, but for now let's look at Fanny Crosby, a woman who wrote many loved hymns. When she was just six weeks old, a cold caused an inflammation of her eyes. The family physician was not home, so a stranger was called. This man recommended the use of hot poultices, which ultimately destroyed her sight.

Crosby wrote,

> When this sad misfortune became known throughout our neighborhood, the unfortunate man thought it best to leave; and we never heard of him again. But I have not for a moment, in more than 85 years, felt a spark of resentment against him because I have always believed from my youth to this very moment that the good Lord, in His infinite mercy, by this means consecrated me to the work that I am still permitted to do.[5]

At eight or nine years of age, while the children her age were preoccupied with jumping rope and playing hopscotch and tag, she penned these words:

> Oh, what a happy soul I am,
> Although I cannot see,
> I am resolved that in this world
> Contented I will be.

How many blessing I enjoy
That other people don't!
To weep and sigh because I'm blind
I cannot nor I won't.[6]

It was a rare day when Fanny Crosby didn't view her blindness as a blessing. However, one hymn, "Hold Thou My Hand," was written when all seemed dark. "That was indeed an unusual experience," she wrote later, "for I have always been most cheerful; and so in my human weakness, I cried in prayer, 'Dear Lord, hold Thou my hand.'"[7] The hymn was so consoling that after Charles Spurgeon's death, his wife wrote for a copy of the poem because she had found comfort from hearing it sung.

Fanny Crosby wrote more than six thousand hymns. Her suffering led her to achieve excellence.

As the saying goes, "We can't control the circumstances of our lives, but we can control our response to our circumstances." This is often the ways God transforms suffering into the seed of excellence. Suffering can bless us and glorify God if we respond to it with faith. Job did. So did Fanny Crosby and thousands of other Christians. We can, too.

Why do we suffer? Every answer I have suggested testifies to the fact that suffering can lead to excellence. Suffering and glory go hand in hand. Christ's death was followed by the glory of His resurrection, establishing the glory we will one day share with Him. Walter Kaiser reminds us that "the most comforting news Scripture has for the sufferer is that where pain, grief, and hurt are, there is God. Instead of a panacea, our Lord offers His presence. One of the greatest promises in the Bible, which speaks to all our fears, is bound up in the very name of our Lord—Immanuel: 'God with us.'"[8]

Life will always include tears. Jesus told us, "In the world you will have tribulation" (John 16:33). But we can excel . . . if we move beyond our tears to the glory that waits us. God promises to make us complete after we "have suffered a while" (see 1 Peter 5:10). Can anyone ask for more?

Good morning, God, I love You! What are You up to today? I want to be part of it.

Missionary Norman Grubb

For all that has been, thanks! For all that shall be, yes!

Dag Hammarskjöld (1905–1961)
Secretary General of United Nations 1953–1960

Our prayers are only as powerful as our lives. In the long pull we pray only as well as we live.

A. W. Tozer (1897–1963)

The one concern of the devil is to keep the saints from praying. He fears nothing from prayerless studies, prayerless work, and prayerless religion. He laughs at our toil, he mocks our wisdom, but he trembles when we pray.

Samuel Chadwick (1832–1917)

Those who have left the deepest impression on this sin-cursed earth have been men and women of prayer.

D. L. Moody (1837–1899)

8

PRAYER—THE LIFELINE TO HEAVEN

Then Jesus told his disciples a parable to show
them that they should always pray and not give up.

Luke 18:1 NIV

"Ask and it will be given to you; seek and you will find;
knock and the door will be opened to you."

Matthew 7:7 NIV

Back in the 1980s, the Pacific Garden Mission of Chicago faced threats of being forced to move from their 107-year-old location. They were told that the mission was drawing undesirable people into the South Loop.

A local news reporter thrust a microphone into the face of Supt. Harry Saulnier and asked, "How do you feel about the city planning board's desires and what is your response? What are you going to do now?"

The white-haired man, his features and slight frame gnarled by rheumatoid arthritis and eighty years of living, didn't lash out or cite legal defense tactics. He didn't refer to the mission's outstanding contributions: the thousands of rehabilitated men and women and their national radio program,

Unshackled, featuring former addicts who tell their stories to inspire others to break their drug and alcohol addiction. Instead he replied, "Well, there's nothing I can do but pray."

The future seemed bleak as he heard the board's plans and they must have been magnified by the news reporters who badgered him with questions. But while his opponents descended on their prey, he descended to his knees to pray.

What happened? Within a few weeks the city put their plans on hold and waited to seek a possible solution. In fact, they waited over a decade before the mission moved to 1455 S. Canal Street, where the mission is prospering under the gifted leadership of Pastor Phil Kwiatkowski, a graduate of both Moody Bible Institute and Liberty University.

Alfred Lord Tennyson once said, "More things are wrought by prayer than this world dreams of." I agree. And so did well-known leaders who changed their generations, people like D. L. Moody, who claimed, "Every great movement of God can be traced to a kneeling figure."

> Prayer enables us to achieve excellence because it changes the events of this world.

Why is prayer important to the pursuit of excellence? The answer is that prayer enables us to achieve excellence because it changes the events of this world. It also changes us; it is God's cure for caving in. We should always pray and never give up, Jesus said (see Luke 18:1).

Jesus did nothing without prayer. He prayed when He was baptized, which began His public ministry. The Father heard these prayers and answered, "You are My beloved Son; in You I am well pleased" (Luke 3:22).

Jesus prayed in the face of decisions. When He set out to select the twelve disciples—the men who would continue His ministry under persecution and pressure—He knew the choice was far too important to make without prayer.

Jesus was known to spend the early morning hours alone in meditation and prayer. He rose a "long while before daylight, . . . He went out and departed to a solitary place; and there He prayed" (Mark 1:35).

If prayer was important for Jesus, the God-Man, how presumptuous to think we can neglect prayer and still excel! "The Lord Jesus is still praying," wrote evangelist S. D. Gordon, who is famous for his twenty-four books in his Quiet Talks series. "Thirty years of living; thirty years of serving; one tremendous act of dying; nineteen hundred years of praying. What an emphasis on prayer!"[1] Jesus believes so completely in the power of prayer that right now He is praying for you and me (see Heb. 7:25).

E. M. Bounds left his secure, settled pastorate to arouse others to the urgent need for prayer. He knew why Christians neglect this essential part of the pursuit of excellence. He wrote,

> Praying is spiritual work; and human nature does not like taxing, spiritual work. Human nature wants to sail to heaven under a favoring breeze, a full, smooth sea. . . . So we come to one of the crying evils of these times, maybe of all times—little or no praying. Of these two evils, perhaps little praying is worse than no praying. Little praying is

kind of make-believe, a salve for the conscience, a farce and a delusion.[2]

Believers of the past shared Bounds's view that prayer is a necessity. D. L. Moody often told of the blessings he received from a dynamic prayer life:

> You know it is when a man is alone with his wife that he tells her the precious secrets of his soul. It is not when the family are around, or when there is company there. So, when we want to get the secrets of heaven we want to be alone with Jesus, and listen that He may come and whisper to our souls. The richest hours I have ever had with God have not been in great assemblies . . . but sitting alone at the feet of Jesus.[3]

KEYS TO EFFECTIVE PRAYER

People sometimes say to me, "I don't feel God's presence when I pray, nor do I get any answers either."

"You won't," I reply, "if you don't work at it." Then I share five keys of effective prayer: humility, obedience, faith, persistence, and concentration.

Humility

Do people ever turn their backs to you when you speak to them? Or ignore you when you need help? Now imagine God turning His back on you when you ask for His help and guidance. That's what happens when we pray without humility. The apostle James wrote, "God resists the proud, but gives grace to the humble" (James 4:6). We must come to God in humility if we want Him to hear. A servant attitude must undergird all that we are and do.

Obedience

The second principle of prayer is obedience. We cannot grow in our praying if we are living carelessly. "If I regard iniquity in my heart, the Lord will not hear," the psalmist warned (Ps. 66:18). Unconfessed sin is disobedience. Sin blocks our communication with God and His spiritual power in our lives. Sin knocks down the power lines.

When we come before God in prayer, we need to remind ourselves of God's throne in heaven. Can we stand before Him without feeling guilty? Prayer should be preceded by this question and begin with our answer to it: a confession of what we have done wrong. We can then approach God humbly and purely, and we can expect Him to answer. Isaiah 1:19 reminds us, "If you are willing and obedient, you will eat the good things of the land" (NIV).

Faith

Before God acts on our prayers, we must have faith that God can answer them. Jesus promised, "Whatever things you ask when you pray, believe that you receive them, and you will have them" (Mark 11:24). It was said of Praying Hyde, a missionary to India, "He prayed as if God were at his elbow," standing ready to answer. He prayed in faith!

Too often our prayers are "milk toast" prayers. We pray, but we think, *Maybe God will do this.* Jacob's attitude was different. When he was going to meet Esau, whose birthright he had stolen, Jacob feared retribution. He asked God, "Deliver me, I pray, from the hand of my brother, from the hand of Esau" (Gen. 32:11). When Jacob didn't receive an answer, he wrestled with God until the breaking of day. Jacob told God, "I will not let You go unless You bless me!" (Gen. 32:26). And God gave Jacob the name Israel, for "you have struggled with God and with men, and have prevailed" (Gen. 32:28).

Jacob wrestled with God because he knew God would save him. He had faith. How many of us really believe God can change events in our lives? How many of us really believe God can change us?

"Jacob's victory of faith could not have been gained without that all-night wrestling," E. M. Bounds observed. "God's acquaintance is not made hurriedly. He does not bestow His gifts on the casual or hasty comer and goer. . . . He yields to the persistency of a faith that knows Him."[4] God cannot answer our prayer if we do not truly believe, if we do not have faith. Without faith—we cannot be saved. Without faith—we cannot grow. Without faith—we cannot please God. Without faith—we cannot receive answers to our prayers.

Persistence

E. M. Bounds said further that God "bestows His richest gifts upon those who declare their desire for and appreciation of those gifts by the constancy as well as earnestness of their importunity."[5] Persistence is the fourth principle of effective prayer.

David repeatedly cried out to God in the Psalms, "Hear my prayer, O God." When his enemies continued to pursue him, and he could not see God's answer, he urged God again, "Give ear to my prayer, O God, and do not hide Yourself from my supplication" (Ps. 55:1). David didn't look for some missing recipe for prayer. He cried out to God in distress. "Hear my prayer, O LORD, and give ear to my cry; do not be silent at my tears" (Ps. 39:12).

David pursued God for help just as persistently as King Saul and his soldiers pursued David—and just as urgently. He believed God could save him. His life depended upon God's answer. David vowed, "Evening and morning and at noon I will pray, and cry aloud" (Ps. 55:17).

We will never know God, we will never hear His answer or receive His help, unless we pursue Him as David did—day in and day out. We must believe, as David did, that our lives depend on prayer.

Concentration

The final principle of prayer is concentration. We need to pray specifically and wisely. We should determine what we really want from God. When I consult my doctor, I carefully prepare a list of questions so all my needs will be considered. Should consultation with God be any different? Many Christians keep a list of prayer requests, and they go through the list specifically when they pray.

Robert Cook tells of a missionary who was evacuated during World War II from a South Pacific island. He was put on a freighter that zigzagged through enemy waters in its journey to safety. One day the periscope of an enemy submarine appeared directly in front of their ship.

"That's when I learned to pray specifically and in detail," said the missionary. "While [the enemy] was looking at us and probably wondering whether or not to sink us, we were praying over every inch of that submarine. 'Lord,' we prayed, 'stop his motors, jam his torpedo tubes, break his rudder!'"[6]

Miraculously, the submarine submerged, never to be confronted again.

Specific prayers can result in miracles, as long as we pray with wisdom. The apostle James warns us, "You ask and do not receive, because you ask amiss, that you may spend it on your pleasures" (James 4:3).

A wife should not pray, "Lord make my husband become a Christian." God doesn't usually work that way. Rather she should pray, "Lord, help me relate to my husband lovingly so he might see You in my daily life."

At the same time, each of us should ask, "Have I done my part? Am I reflecting God's love in my life?" If someone prays for a job, he must be willing to read the want ads and go to interview after interview for weeks and months. The Lord always expects us to do our part.

Humility, obedience, faith, persistence, and concentration are essential to effective prayer, which accompanies excellence. When we pray with our whole hearts and souls and minds, we join the prophets of old whose prayers accomplished miracles.

WHAT HAPPENS WHEN PEOPLE PRAY?

Scripture describes the prophet Elijah as "a man with a nature like ours" (James 5:17). What happened when Elijah prayed earnestly that it would not rain? A three-year drought descended upon Israel! What happened when he prayed for the widow's son? The boy came back to life! What happened when he prayed during a contest with the prophets of Baal to determine whose God was real? An altar, which had been doused with water three times, broke into flame! Prayer leads to miracles. Prayer leads to excellence—not only in the Bible but in the lives of God's people today.

In the first years of my administration at Moody Bible Institute, we experienced such rapid growth in so many areas that we needed additional office space. Bob Constable, our Executive Vice President, came to me in desperation and asked, "What can we do?" I suggested that we immediately kneel in prayer asking the Lord to show us His will. That very day, I received a phone call from A. C. Nelson offering us a five story office building on Howard Street, valued at two million dollars, on the condition that we would use it and not sell it for at least three years. Needless to say, we were exceedingly grateful and used this building for many years. This is what happens when people pray.

On Easter Sunday in 1946, along with 60,000 other people, I attended a sunrise service in Chicago's Soldier Field. The sky was dark, and it was already raining to the east over Lake Michigan.

Harry Saulnier introduced Charles E. Fuller of the *Old*

Fashioned Revival Hour. Immediately he told the audience, "It's not going to rain, and I'm not even going to put my hat on," and for the next hour, it did not rain!

He closed his message with an invitation for people to receive Jesus Christ, and hundreds responded. After the stadium emptied and the audience were well on their way home, the rain come down torrentially! This is what happens when people pray.

Nothing is too big and nothing is too small to pray about.

Second Chronicles 16:9 promises us, "The eyes of the LORD range throughout the earth to strengthen those whose hearts are fully committed to him" (NIV).

Prayer is our lifeline to heaven.

E. M. Bounds interpreted 2 Chronicles 16:9 in this way:

When God declares that "the eyes of the Lord run to and from throughout the whole earth, to shew himself strong in the behalf of them whose heart is perfect toward him" (2 Chronicles 16:9), He declares the necessity of men and His dependence on them as a channel through which to exert His power upon the world. . . . What the Church needs today is not more machinery or better, not new organizations or more and novel methods, but men whom the Holy Spirit can use.[7]

E. M. Bounds continues, "We are 'the eyes of the Lord.'" He is looking to us to bring the concerns of His people before Him. Prayer is a vital experience in our pursuit of excellence. It is the life line between earth and heaven. Any army is stranded without its short-wave radios, walkie-talkies, and computers. God's army is no different. Prayer provides the instant communication and the ultimate power to enable us to accomplish His excellent work here on earth.

Do you see a person wise in their own eyes?
There is more hope for a fool than for them.

Proverbs 26:12 NIV

Not for a single day
Can I discern my way,
But this I surely know—
Who gives the day
Will show the way,
So I securely go.

John Oxenham

I have been driven many times to my knees by the overwhelming
conviction that I had nowhere else to go. My own wisdom, and that of
all about me, seemed insufficient for the day.

Abraham Lincoln

Wisdom is the principal thing; therefore get wisdom.

Proverbs 4:7 KJV

9

WISDOM—THE ETERNAL PERSPECTIVE

For the LORD gives wisdom; from his mouth
come knowledge and understanding.

Proverbs 2:6 NIV

Who is wise and understanding among you? Let them show
it by their good life, by deeds done in the humility that comes
from wisdom. . . . But the wisdom that comes from heaven is
first of all pure; then peace-loving, considerate, submissive, full
of mercy and good fruit, impartial and sincere. Peacemakers
who sow in peace reap a harvest of righteousness.

James 3:13, 17–18 NIV

The old saying "Do as I say, not as I do" captures the essence
of life, the enigma people have faced throughout the ages: the
inability to translate the truth they know into the actions of
everyday life. Paul said it this way: "What I will to do, that I
do not practice; but what I hate, that I do" (Rom. 7:15).

To me, wisdom is the ability to know what is right—to
be able to discern between good and evil—and then to translate that knowledge into everyday living. A look at the life
of Solomon, the wisest man who ever lived, is a case study in
how to obtain wisdom, how to act on that wisdom, and sad to

say, how to finally lose it. By observing Solomon's success and failures, we can learn how to experience God's wisdom.

CHOOSE WISDOM

None of us can begin better than Solomon did. When he assumed the throne of Israel, he intuitively knew wisdom was a core ingredient of excellence. When the Lord appeared to Solomon in a dream and said, "Ask! What shall I give you?" (1 Kings 3:5), Solomon chose wisdom.

Put yourself in Solomon's place. If God told you He would give you whatever you asked for, how would you respond? Would you answer, "A new house"? "A car"? "A boat"? Or would you be less selfish and request, "A new three-thousand-seat sanctuary for my church family"? What about the intangible items of love, faith, goodness, or wisdom?

Solomon chose wisdom. Even though he was a new king, he replied,

I am a little child; I do not know how to go out or come in. And [I am] in the midst of Your people whom You have chosen, a great people, too numerous to be numbered or counted. Therefore give to Your servant an understanding heart to judge Your people, that I may discern between good and evil. (1 Kings 3:7–9)

Solomon realized his inadequacy and the severity of the task he had to accomplish. He asked for wisdom before he began to rule the Israelites, not after he had made poor decisions and was about to be ousted. We, too, are told to humbly seek the Lord for wisdom (see James 1:5).

KNOW THE KEY TO WISDOM

In the book of Proverbs, Solomon spoke of how to live a godly life here one earth and how to be ready for the life to come. "Listen," Solomon said, "for I will speak of excellent things" (Prov. 8:6).

The key to wisdom, Solomon maintained, is simply to keep God's commandments. Solomon didn't dream up this rule. God told him about it over and over again, just as He had told his father, David, before him: "If you . . . do according to all that I have commanded you, and if you keep My statutes and My judgments, then I will establish the throne of your kingdom over Israel forever" (1 Kings 9:4–5).

"Do not forget, nor turn away from the words of my mouth," Solomon cautioned (Prov. 4:5). Just because we start to follow God's commandments doesn't guarantee that we will always follow them. Solomon was unable to follow his own advice. Why?

Solomon broke God's commandment: "You shall not intermarry with [other nations], nor they with you. Surely they will turn away your hearts after their gods" (1 Kings 11:2).

This error lay dormant during much of Solomon's reign, but as he grew older it began to manifest itself. I imagine Solomon neglected to read God's Word, just as those of us who fail to achieve excellence forget to read the Scriptures. He was probably surrounded by fawning aides who gave him plenty of advice and gushed over his wisdom, so he forgot that his wisdom was God's gift to him, not a natural part of his personality. Solomon broke God's commandment again and again; he married seven hundred women from other nations. How tragic! He began so well and ended so poorly.

When Solomon was old, he began to accept his pagan wives' gods: Ashtoreth, Milcom, Chemosh, Molech. You name the god, and Solomon built an altar to it so that his foreign wives could worship. Soon he joined his wives in their worship and broke the first commandment, "You shall have no other gods before Me" (Ex. 20:3).

Once you start to disobey, a pattern is established that is painfully hard to break. What is your watershed? What commandment are you tempted to break? Beware of it because it will keep you from lasting excellence, just as disobedience and lust corrupted Solomon.

SEE LIFE FROM GOD'S PERSPECTIVE

Solomon is the prime example of someone unable to translate the knowledge he has into the actions of a lifetime. As an old man, a disillusioned Solomon looked back on his life and declared all the riches, all the power, all the pleasures of wine and laughter, all the words of his life as vanity. He admitted, "I did not withhold my heart from any pleasure. . . . All was vanity and grasping for the wind. There was no profit under the sun" (Eccl. 2:10–11).

How do we gain a divine perspective? Those of us who have stood beside friends and loved ones as they lay dying have felt the futility Solomon suggested in his writings: the brevity of our lives and the frailness of our human bodies. The inability to talk or eat or breathe on our own is something many of us will someday face. What will seem important to us then? The money we have in the bank? The times we failed and felt we could never succeed?

None of the above. Only what is true and eternal will matter. Is this not the peephole through which we are to view every day of our lives? Is this not the yardstick for wise decision-making? Is this not the framework for a divine perspective?

Francis Schaeffer was a man who saw life from this perspective. He conformed to God's Word, not to the world around him. His resistance to social pressures was often obvious in his dress; he unabashedly wore lederhosen among men in gray flannel suits and young adults in jeans. But what really made Schaeffer different was his philosophy, which challenged people to return to God's eternal truths and standards. Schaeffer called everyone to see the ethical issues of his century—abortion, euthanasia, practicing homosexuality, promiscuous sex—from God's perspective and realize they are morally wrong. He was not afraid to stand for God's truth, even against the church itself.

Schaeffer chastised lukewarm Christians for neglecting to represent God's views in this ethical battle. He wrote, "When it comes to the issues of the day the evangelical world most often has said nothing; or worse has said nothing different from what the world would say. Here is the great evangelical disaster—the failure of the evangelical world to stand for truth as truth."[1]

Christians have to disagree with the world when ultimate truth is involved, Schaeffer said, but always in love: "Lovingly marking visibly where that line falls, lovingly showing that some are on the other side of the line, and making clear to everyone on both sides of the line what the consequences of this are."[2] Schaeffer's wise belief in God's love as the mark of the Christian kept his voice from being too strident; instead of the sharpness of a knife, which destroys, his words were meant as polish for the church's rough edges.

Schaeffer was rebuffed. He was criticized. He was ridiculed as the "evangelical guru." But he persisted. Why? Because he strove to please only the Lord of his life, who was his everyday friend, whom he would soon meet face-to-face. He tried to see this world from God's perspective and the peephole of eternity.

Schaeffer said,

It is my firm belief that when we stand before Jesus Christ, we will find that it has been the weakness and accommodation of the evangelical group on the issues of the day that has been largely responsible for the loss of the Christian ethos which has taken place in the area of culture in our own country over the last forty to sixty years.[3]

Only God knows if Francis Schaeffer was right, but he was undoubtedly a man of wisdom. He never forgot God. He continually strove to keep God's commandments in every area of his life.

REFLECT WISDOM

The apostle James suggested that a person who is wise reflects wisdom in his daily deeds (see James 3:13), just as Schaeffer did. James contrasted earthly wisdom and heavenly wisdom, so we can discern the difference. He said, "If you have bitter envy and self-seeking in your hearts, do not boast and lie against the truth. This wisdom does not descend from above, but is earthly, sensual, demonic. For where envy and self-seeking exist, confusion and every evil thing are there" (James 3:14–16).

Heavenly wisdom is "first pure, then peaceable, gentle, willing to yield, full of mercy and good fruits, without partiality and without hypocrisy" (James 3:17). You are not wise, no matter what you may claim, unless your everyday life reflects these characteristics.

Are people afraid to disagree with you because an opposing word will make you angry and inattentive? Are you open to change if better views than yours are presented?

Often our churches lack this openness. When fresh biblical ideas are introduced by a new member, they are squelched. Such closed-mindedness on the part of church leaders fails to reflect heavenly wisdom.

James spoke of heavenly wisdom as being "full of mercy and good fruits" (James 3:17). This means your works should back up your words. True wisdom is not marked by hypocrisy. Are you partial toward certain people, or do you give everyone equal consideration? God in His perfect wisdom doesn't view you in a racial or economic class or in an echelon of spirituality. He has warned you not to prefer the wealthy or prestigious to those who seem poor, for He has chosen the poor of this world to be rich in faith and heirs of the kingdom (see James 2:1–9).

THE BENEFITS OF WISDOM

Few of us could want much more than the blessings Solomon found to accompany wisdom. He built a great temple for God, a palace for himself, and another for the daughter of Pharaoh, and protective walls for such cities as Jerusalem, Hazor, Megiddo, and Gezer. He had so many chariots and such a large cavalry that he had to build storage cities to house them. He "made silver as common in Jerusalem as stones" (1 Kings 10:27). The queen of Sheba sought Solomon's presence to hear his wisdom (see 1 Kings 10:1–13).

The blessings of wisdom were so abundant that Solomon said, "Happy is the man who finds wisdom" (Prov. 3:13). "You will walk safely in your way, and your foot will not stumble. When you lie down, you will not be afraid" (Prov. 3:23–24). Within wisdom are happiness, security, honor, and riches all at once.

God kept His promises to Solomon. With God's help, Solomon united Israel into an empire that stretched from the Euphrates River on the north to Egypt on the south, from the Mediterranean Sea on the west to the Arabian Desert on the east.

But Solomon did not keep his part of the bargain. He failed to end well. He forgot that the prize is at the end of the journey. God warned Solomon, "But if you or your sons at all turn from following Me, and do not keep My commandments

. . . but go and serve other gods and worship them, then I will cut off Israel from the land which I have given them" (1 Kings 9:6–7). After Solomon's death the great nation he had built split into two kingdoms, never to recapture the glory of Solomon's reign.

Solomon concluded the book of Ecclesiastes with two great admonitions: "Remember your Creator" and "Fear God and keep his commandments, for this is the duty of all mankind" (Eccl. 12:1, 13 NIV). Solomon learned his lesson too late to change the course of history. Instead he challenged us: Do as I say, not as I did. Remember God! Keep His commandments! You shall be wiser than I. You shall know the joy of ending well. For the end of a thing is more important than its beginning.

Wisdom is an important mark of excellence, but as is true for the other attributes, it alone is insufficient. Wisdom must be accompanied by faith, character, action, single-mindedness, love, prayer, suffering, and staying power. Solomon lacked staying power, the mark of excellence I will explore in the next chapter.

Each of us has the opportunity to end well. Francis Schaeffer will never be called "the wisest man who ever lived," as Solomon was. But Schaeffer, a man like you and me, ended well. He fought the fight. He obeyed God's commandments. He saw life from God's perspective. Each book he wrote, each speech he gave, stood for truth and righteousness in a fallen world. Francis Schaeffer was only one of God's choice servants. God is calling you and me to join him, to commit our lives to excellence.

And they continued steadfastly in the apostles' doctrine and fellowship, in the breaking of bread, and in prayers.

Acts 2:42

O Lord, when you give to your servants to endeavor any great matter grant us also to know, that it is not the beginning but the continuing of the same, until it be thoroughly finished, which yields the true glory; through Him who, for the finishing of Your work, laid down His life.

Based on a letter by Sir Francis Drake (1540–1596)

Now it is required that those who have been given a trust must prove faithful.

1 Corinthians 4:2 NIV

10

STAYING POWER—THE ENDURANCE TO END WELL

*Through the Lord's mercies we are not consumed,
because His compassions fail not. They are
new every morning; great is Your faithfulness.*

Lamentations 3:22–23

*When Jesus had received the sour wine, He said,
"It is finished!" And bowing His head, He gave up His spirit.*

John 19:30

"I have fought the good fight, I have finished the race, I have kept the faith" (2 Tim. 4:7 NIV).

Years ago Pastor Russell Conwell told the story of an ancient Persian, Ali Hafed, in the classic *Acres of Diamonds*: "Ali Hafed owned a very large farm . . . he had orchards, grainfields, and gardens . . . and was a wealthy and contented man."

One day a Buddhist priest from the East told the old farmer all about diamonds and about how wealthy he would be if he owned a diamond mine. Ali Hafed went to bed that night a poor man, poor because he was discontented. He craved a mine of diamond. Soon he sold his farm and began an endless search for the rare stones. He traveled the world over, and he finally became so poor, broken, and defeated that he committed suicide. He did not have staying power.

One day the man who purchased Ali Hafed's farm led his camel into the garden to drink. As his camel put its nose into the shallow water of the garden brook, the farmer noticed a curious flash of light from the white sands of the stream. He pulled out a black stone that had an eye of light, which reflected all the hues of the rainbow. A diamond!

The man had discovered

the diamond mine of Golcanda, the most significant diamond mine in the history of mankind, excelling the Kimberly itself. . . .

Had Ali Hafed remained at home and dug in his own cellar, or underneath his own wheat fields, or in his own garden, instead of wretchedness, starvation, and death by suicide in a strange land, he would have had "acres of diamonds." For every acre of that old farm, yes, every shovelful, afterward revealed gems which since have decorated the crowns of monarchs.[1]

I enjoyed the friendship of Paul Harvey, the national news commentator. Yearly, he would call me in December to secure reservations for Moody's Christmas program, "Candlelight Carols." We were honored to have the Harvey family.

On one occasion, he devoted most of his daily broadcast to praising the Moody Bible Institute for staying in the city of Chicago. Harvey spoke on the subject of "Bloom Where You're Planted."

He spoke of the acres of diamonds in downtown Chicago.

He commended the Moody Bible Institute for staying power, for blooming where the school was planted in 1886. Chicago has been a great city in which to serve and fulfill our mission.

For many years I traveled as an itinerant evangelist. Regardless of the geographic location—sunny California or windy Chicago—the majority of people I encountered were restless and discontented with life. They were continually looking for greener pastures.

Pastors often would ask tactfully if I knew of some strategic church, worthy of their talents, that was looking for a gifted minister. "Yes," I would answer thoughtfully and then put off giving them details. In the next days, I would do everything within my power to show these friends the promise of their present opportunities, their acres of diamonds. By the end of the week, they were usually so excited about the potential of their own ministries that they forgot to ask about that mythical, perfect church somewhere. They had found staying power.

What is staying power? Some call it perseverance. Others might add old-fashioned steadiness, faithfulness, and consistency. Not enough is said today about hanging in there until the job is done, about finishing well.

My predecessor at the Moody Bible Institute, William Culbertson, occasionally said, "My prayer for you and for myself is that we end well." October 6, 1971, he entered Swedish Covenant Hospital for the third time in ten years. Lung cancer had returned, and treatment was given. On November 16, he was bright and hopeful of recovery, but that was not to be. That evening he quoted a favorite phrase from Revelation 19:6, "Allelujah: for the Lord God omnipotent reigneth" (KJV).

Shortly after, he spoke his last words, "God—God, yes!" His prayer, to end well, was answered.

Our world argues against longevity. "Our attention spans have been conditioned by thirty-second commercials. Our sense of reality has been flattened by thirty-page abridgments," says Eugene Peterson in *A Long Obedience in the Same Direction.* Peterson continues,

> Millions of people in our culture make decisions for Christ, but there is a dreadful attrition rate. . . . In our kind of culture anything, even news about God, can be sold if it is packaged freshly; but when it loses its novelty, it goes on the garbage heap. There is a great market for religious experience in our world; there is little enthusiasm for the patient acquisition of virtue, little inclination to sign up for a long apprenticeship.[2]

It's the long, steady apprenticeship that counts, as we learned from Solomon's tragedy at the end of the last chapter. Solomon did not end well, but our Christian forefathers did. We can learn a great deal about staying power by observing the principles that directed the apostolic church. The early Christians knew their purpose. They were guided by Jesus' last words, "You shall be witnesses to Me in Jerusalem, and in all Judea and Samaria, and to the end of the earth" (Acts 1:8). They accepted the Great Commission as their supreme task. None of us can have staying power until we have established the lifetime goals I suggested in chapter 5.

The first-century Christians acted on their goal immediately after they received the power of the Holy Spirit. Peter told the multitude that came to investigate the happenings at Pentecost about Jesus Christ. That small band of Christians had a bias for action.

Then came their perseverance. Day after day, month after month, for years and years after Christ ascended into heaven, "they continued steadfastly in the apostles' doctrine and fellowship, in the breaking of bread, and in prayers" (Acts 2:42). "They continued steadfastly." I like that. They were steady. Reliable. Loyal. Faithful. You could count on them, come what may.

The servants of Jesus are told to "be found faithful" (1 Cor. 4:2). Faithfulness is required, not merely recommended. God does not require us to be successful, but He does require us to be faithful. If we want to have staying power, we must remain steadfast in obedience, fellowship, and doctrine, despite any ridicule or persecution we might receive.

STEADFAST OBEDIENCE

Unlike Solomon, the early Christians remained obedient to God's commandments. They did what God told them no matter how impossible or unusual it seemed. Imagine how Ananias must have felt when God told him to help Saul, who was a notorious persecutor of Christians. It must have been like God telling the Jews in Germany to rescue a member of the SS or Hitler himself.

But when God said, "Go, for he is a chosen vessel of Mine to bear My name before Gentiles, kings, and the children of Israel" (Acts 9:15), Ananias immediately obeyed.

So do many Christians today, ordinary men and women like you and me who choose to do God's will, regardless of the cost. During the first 130 years of the Moody Bible Institute, over six thousand students have become missionaries to spread the good news to other lands, despite the threat of persecution. More than twenty graduates of Moody Bible Institute have been martyred, men and women like John and Betty Stam.

I knew most of the Stam family personally. John's brother Jacob, a lawyer, was a close and special friend to me. His brother Henry, an outstanding realtor, was a member of the church I pastored. I knew and greatly appreciated their families.

While I spoke at America's Keswick conference in Whiting, New Jersey, the director showed me copy of Betty Scott Stam's teenage decision card. Here are her exact words,

Lord, I give up all my own plans and purposes, all my own desires and hopes, and accept thy will for my life. I give myself, my life, my all utterly to you, to be Thine forever. Fill me with the Holy Spirit. Use me as Thou wilt. Send me where Thou wilt. Work out Thy whole will in my life at any cost now and forever.

—Signed Betty Scott, age 13

John Stam knew the risk he was taking when he went to China. His father had protested, "Why think of China or India, when there are other countries more open? Would it not seem more in keeping with the Lord's will to go where work can be unhindered, rather than where life is always in danger and there is so much opposition?"[3]

In the early 1930s, Communist armies were in possession of the larger part of Kiangsi province and were killing all who opposed them. Three associate members of the China Inland Mission (now Overseas Missionary Fellowship) had been murdered and two others were being held prisoner, but John could picture the scores of cities in China that did not have the gospel. He knew God was calling him to the harvest there, and his father finally agreed with him. John Stam was obedient to God, regardless of the danger. In 1932, he and his wife, Betty, sailed for China, despite the growing threat from Communist forces who captured city after city.

We, too, must obey God to receive the power to persevere. Some call this blind faith, but it is blind only in the sense that we can't see God face-to-face. Like John and Betty, hundreds of us today have experienced God's Spirit guiding us. His presence is real. Our faith is not blind. We obey the Holy Spirit of God within us.

STEADFAST FELLOWSHIP

Another key to the early Christians' staying power was fellowship, the strengthening of one another. They could count on one another, just as they could count on the Lord. No one went hungry or without shelter.

When the Christians in Antioch heard about the famine in Jerusalem, they didn't just say, "Oh, that's so sad!" and pray for the Lord's help. They sent Paul and Barnabas to Jerusalem with money to buy food for their starving brothers and sisters.

God calls us to help one another in such ways. We may

not literally pool our possessions, but we can figuratively hold them in common. If I see a friend suffering, someone who has lost a job and needs money to keep the family going in tough times, I should share my money with my friend. I am not loaning this friend money; it is part of my gift to the Lord who has guided me to use it in this way.

Christian caring is more than financial aid. It is crying with someone whose husband or daughter is dying. It is laughing together when that same person remarries or has another child. When Dorcas became sick and died, the disciples at Joppa sent two men to nearby Lydda to get Peter and ask him to heal their sister in Christ. All the widows were standing beside her bed when he arrived. Peter answered their request and raised Dorcas from the dead (see Acts 9:36–43).

God calls us to care for one another and to sustain one another. We are not meant to face this alien world alone; we are meant to face it together. By working in union, we share His power and love so that we all can persevere.

STEADFAST DOCTRINE

The early Christians were steadfast in doctrine. They knew what they believed, they practiced that belief day in and day out, and they constantly contended for the faith. Peter wrote that we should always "be ready to give a defense to everyone who asks [us] a reason for the hope that is in [us], with meekness and fear" (1 Peter 3:15).

Paul reminded us to fight "the good fight of faith" (1 Tim. 6:12). Each generation must in turn fight that good fight and keep the faith. We are always only one generation away from the eclipse of the faith, because God doesn't have any grandchildren. In our day, we too need to be steadfast in doctrine.

We all need to be missionaries like John and Betty Stam, whether we journey to far-off lands or remain at home. The Stams were dedicated to spreading the good news of Jesus Christ. No one was sure that their special parish in southern Anhwei was safe. John and Betty visited it together in February of 1934, and John again visited the district that fall. At first the district magistrate warned him not to come, but later in the conversation he stated that the district was quiet and would be safe for John, his wife, and their small baby.

John was torn between worry and his desire to spread the gospel. However, if he waited until all was assuredly peaceful, he felt the present generation of Chinese would never hear the gospel. He took his family to the little city of Tsingteh, the center of Anhwei. John was ready to answer the Chinese people's natural hunger for God, regardless of the consequences.

STEADFAST COURAGE

Rain, wind, storm, and persecution couldn't turn the early Christians away from their purpose. Suppose you were like Peter or John and were jailed for healing a lame beggar and preaching Jesus' resurrection. The next day you would have to face all the rulers, elders, and scribes of the temple—the Senate of the United States, maybe, or in John and Betty Stam's case, the Red Army. Would you claim some special power? Would you deny the man's healing so that you could be set free? Would you give up your Christian faith?

Peter did none of these things. Instead, he boldly proclaimed the source of his power, Jesus Christ. Only through Him can you be saved, Peter said. When the council demanded that the disciples never speak the name of Jesus again, Peter and John answered, "Whether it is right in the sight of God to listen to you more than to God, you judge" (Acts 4:19).

The two disciples put the threats of this world in perspective. To whom would they listen? God, of course. Later when they were again imprisoned on the same charge, they gave the same answer to the high priest, "We ought to obey God rather than men" (Acts 5:29).

Many Christians answer this question the same way today. They refuse to accept the immorality and standards of our society, even though their refusal isolates them. Young Christians are ridiculed because they don't practice premarital sex and because they don't use alcohol or drugs. For Betty and John Stam, persecution meant more than ridicule; the balance in China hung precariously between life and death.

In December of 1934, the Red forces attacked the city of Tsingteh. With scarcely any warning, advance guards scaled the city wall, threw open the gates for the rest of the army, and began firing before anyone could escape. Many were killed. Others, including John and Betty and their tiny baby, were captured by the Communists and forced to march with the army to the next target, Miaosheo.

The next day John and Betty Stam were "led up a little hill outside the town. There, in a clump of pine trees, the communists harangued the unwilling onlookers, who were too terror-stricken to utter protest. But one man, a doctor, fell on his knees and pleaded for his friends' lives. At first the Reds tried to push him out of the way. When he persisted, he was dragged off.

John Stam begged the leader to release the man, but John was quickly ordered to kneel, and he was executed. His wife "was seen to quiver, but only for a moment. Bound as she was, she fell on her knees beside him. Another flash of a sword, which mercifully she did not see—and they were reunited."[4]

Their baby, who was not yet three months old, lay sleeping in an empty house where her mother had left her. No one in the village dared go to her. Two days passed. Finally, the Christian evangelist the Stams were working with, Mr. Lo, came to investigate the rumor that two foreigners had been publicly executed.

After much questioning, an old woman finally whispered that the foreign baby was alive and pointed to the house. Mr. Lo and his wife hid the infant and their own child in two large rice baskets and carried them across a hundred miles of mountainous country, filled with bandits and Communist soldiers, to freedom.

> A person may have character, faith, and other marks of excellence, but if he does not have staying power, he accomplishes very little.

Nothing kept the Stams from their witness for Christ in China. They earnestly obeyed God's call and His commandments. They remained steadfast in doctrine, despite persecution. Only death silenced their testimony.[5]

Staying power leads to excellence not only for the missionary or pastor but also for the business person or homemaker. A person may have character, faith, and other marks of excellence, but if he does not have staying power, he accomplishes very little. In times of adversity, he wilts like a cut flower in the sun.

STEADFAST EXAMPLE

Jesus is our primary example of staying power. As a child, He tarried in Jerusalem after the Passover so that He could listen and question leaders in the temple. When His parents rebuked Him, He answered, "Did you not know that I must be about My Father's business?" (Luke 2:49).

He repeatedly stated His sovereign purpose, "I must work the works of Him who sent Me" (John 9:4). When He shared His destiny with His disciples, He rejected Peter's attempt to dissuade Him from the cross: "Get behind Me, Satan! . . . You are not mindful of the things of God, but the things of men" (Matt. 16:23). Jesus corrected Peter's perspective to align it with God's, and his ministry showed that he learned his lesson well.

Even when Jesus was hanging on the cross, wounded and bleeding, He rejected the crowd's cries, "Save Yourself, and come down from the cross!" (Mark 15:30). It's human to let go and come down . . . but it is divine to hang there. Jesus, while on the cross, received the sponge with vinegar, and said, "'It is finished!' And bowing His head, He gave up His spirit" (John 19:30).

Too many people are letting go, coming down, and quitting. How sad it must be to face the Lord and know that you did not finish triumphantly! You fought faithfully for ten or twenty years, just as Solomon did, but in the end, you gave up. You quit. You lost, and that can never be changed.

Jesus set an altogether different example for us. It takes courage to follow His example, and it's not easy; but we, like our early Christian forefathers, can have staying power. The keys are steadfast obedience, fellowship, and doctrine.

What reward do we receive for this staying power? The apostle Peter, who endured years of persecution and was finally crucified upside down for his belief, wrote, "May the God of all grace . . . after you have suffered a while, perfect, establish, strength, and settle you" (1 Peter 5:10).

We shall be given the mastery. We shall experience excellence. We shall be like Jesus—but only after the waiting, the perseverance, and the faithfulness. Having staying power is hard, but it will mature us.

The Jews in Thessalonica dragged Jason and other early Christians to the rulers of the city, proclaiming, "These who have turned the world upside down have come here, too" (Acts 17:6). "Watch out!" they cried, "these men have power! They will destroy our city." They were afraid because the Christians were known for the power of their witness, for their steadfastness in doctrine despite persecution. They gave the early Christians the greatest tribute of all: "They can change the world."

Staying power is an indispensable mark of excellence. It can make the difference. Staying power can change our world.

His sermons were colloquial, simple, full of conviction and point. In his theology he laid stress on the Gospel, not on a sectarian opinion. His intense sympathy for, and insight into the individual, his infinite practical skill and tact, his genius for organization, his honesty, his singular largeness and sweetness of spirit and his passion for mending and winning souls made him, in spite of his scholastic defects, one of the greatest of modern evangelists.

Encyclopedia Britannica (1953 edition), Concerning D. L. Moody

Organization was not preeminently Mr. Moody's endowment. Founding, evangelizing and quick execution were emphatically his. . . . He was, like Elijah, a divinely equipped "flying artillery" on life's battlefield. He broke the enemy's centers and in so doing, incidentally aroused new organizers and was an inspiration to their constructive work.

Emma Dryer, Letter from Emma Dryer to Charles Blanchard, January 1916

Millions of dollars passed into Mr. Moody's hands, but they passed through; they did not stick to his fingers.

R. A. Torrey, *Why God Used D. L. Moody*

11

STEPS OF EXCELLENCE IN THE LIFE OF D. L. MOODY

The world has yet to see what God can do with
and for and through and in a man who is fully
and wholly consecrated to Him.

Henry Varley

The world and its desires pass away,
but whoever does the will of God lives forever.

1 John 2:17 NIV, D. L. Moody's life verse

Finally, brethren, whatever things are true, whatever
things are noble, whatever things are just, whatever things
are pure, whatever things are lovely, whatever things are
of good report, if there is any virtue and if there is anything
praiseworthy—meditate on these things.

Philippians 4:8

When I began to search for the marks of excellence in the lives
of well-known Christian leaders, D. L. Moody, the founder
of Moody Bible Institute, was one of the first examples I
studied. Moody Bible Institute inherited its commitment to
excellence from this spiritual forefather.

What an inspiration I discovered! Moody was like most
of us. The word "genius" was not mentioned by those who described him. Instead they saw attributes that we could emulate:

faith, action, prayer, single-mindedness, and God's love.

This man, who has been called the most famous Protestant clergyman of the nineteenth century, was an unordained layman who had no more than a questionable fifth-grade education. He began life, like many people in our country today, with only the barest Christian understanding. Only God could have transformed a teenager nicknamed "crazy Moody" because of his impetuous nature into a dynamic evangelist.

Few people who knew Moody in 1856 would have dreamed the young man would achieve such excellence. His own uncle tried not to give him a job in his Boston shoe store because of Moody's reputation for brashness and practical joking. One day Moody suddenly appeared at his uncle's shop, after making the long trip from his home in Northfield, Massachusetts, on pure speculation that he would be hired. Samuel Holton refused to employ the young man. But Moody persevered. Holton finally gave in after Moody spent several unsuccessful weeks searching for a job and threatened to move on. Holton made two stipulations. Moody had to attend church and Sunday school and promise not go anywhere at night that he wouldn't tell his mother about.

Moody kept his promise. He was in the Mount Vernon Congregational Church on Sundays, but he often nodded off to sleep during the sermon so that some stern-faced deacon had to poke him awake. His first days in Sunday school were just as awkward. Edward Kimball, his teacher, handed Moody a Bible and told him the lesson was in the gospel of John. The other boys in the class eyed one another as Moody fumbled through the Bible, trying to find the proper page.

One day Edward Kimball visited Moody at Holton's store. The young man was in the back, wrapping and shelving shoes. After the opening amenities, Kimball put his hand on Moody's shoulder and, with tears in his eyes, told Moody of Christ's love for him.

"I had not felt that I had a soul 'til then," Moody later admitted. "I said to myself, 'This is a very strange thing. Here is a man who never saw me till lately, and he is weeping over my sins, and I never shed a tear about them!'"

In the back of that shoe store in Boston, the future great evangelist gave himself to Christ.[1] Moody's act of faith was his first step in his journey to excellence, but he had little biblical knowledge to support his religious experience and his desire to serve God.

He spoke so ungrammatically and offensively in one church meeting that he was asked to keep silent. Such experiences made Moody long for a greater freedom of action and speech; so, in 1856, he bought a five-dollar train ticket to seek his fortune in Chicago. He found a job in a shoe store, and soon he became known as the best shoe salesman in the city.

Moody became interested in the Sunday school work at Chicago's Plymouth Street Church, but he felt unqualified to teach. Instead, he rented four pews and undertook to fill them with young men for the Sunday services.[2] After working for some time in this way, Moody began a mission school, which continually increased in numbers because of Moody's hard work and zeal. He "devoted all of his free time to the work, staying out on the streets at nights until ten or eleven o'clock. People throughout the slum area came to know him.

He enticed children by the promise of sweets drawn from an inexhaustible supply in an inside pocket." One friend called this supply his "missionary sugar."[3]

Moody soon became caught in the game of statistics. When his growing Sunday school attendance dropped below 1,000 he was depressed. When it went up to 1,200 or 1,500 he was elated. Yet few were converted. There was no harvest until God showed Moody the importance of people rather than numbers.

> There was no harvest until God showed Moody the importance of people rather than numbers.

One day a Sunday school teacher fell ill and asked Moody to teach his class, a group Moody described as "without exception the most frivolous set of girls I ever met. . . . They laughed in my face, and I felt like opening the door and telling them all to get out and never come back."[4]

Later that week the teacher stopped by the shoe store to talk to Moody. "I have had another hemorrhage of my lungs," the teacher said. "The doctor says I cannot live on Lake Michigan, so I am going to New York state. I suppose I am going home to die."

Moody sensed that something else was troubling the man; he asked what it was. "Well, I have never led any of my class to Christ," the man confided. "I really believe I have done the girls more harm than good."

"Suppose you go and tell them how you feel," Moody suggested.

Moody later wrote,

He consented, and we started out together. It was one of the best journeys I ever had on earth. We went to the house of one of the girls . . . and the teacher talked to her about her soul. There was no laughing then! Tears stood in her eyes before long. After he had explained the way of life, he suggested that we have prayer. He asked me to pray. True, I had never done such a thing in my life as to pray God to convert a young lady there and then. But we prayed, and God answered our prayer.[5]

For the next ten days, Moody and the teacher visited home after home, both together and separately. It wasn't long before the teacher returned to the shoe store to tell Moody the last girl in his class had yielded herself to Christ.

Without any prior arrangements, the entire class arrived at the train depot the evening the teacher left town. "What a meeting that was!" Moody said,

We tried to sing, but we broke down. The last we saw of that dying teacher he was standing on the platform of the rear car, his finger pointing upward, telling us to meet him in heaven. . . . I had got a taste of another world, and cared no more for making money. For some days after, the greatest struggle of my life took place. Should I give up business and give myself wholly to Christian work, or should I not? . . . I have never regretted my choice.[6]

Moody single-mindedly chose to pursue God's work, another step in his journey to excellence.

If we could ask Moody what led him to excel, I think he would reply, "A real knowledge of God's love and single-minded devotion to serve Him." Love was the mark of excellence that characterized Moody's ministry.

LOVE

Henry Moorehouse, who was called "the boy preacher from England," inspired Moody to pursue God's love with the same kind of fervor I described in chapter 6.

Moorehouse preached at Moody's church as part of a tour of America, but Moody happened to be out of town at the time. The first question Moody asked his wife, Emma, when he returned to Chicago, was, "How is the young [Englishman] coming along? . . . Did you like him?"

"Yes, very much," she replied. "He has preached two sermons from John 3:16, 'For God so loved the world, that he gave his only begotten Son, that whosoever believeth in him should not perish, but have everlasting life'; and I think you will like him, although he preaches a little differently from what you do."

"How is that?"

"Well, he tells the worst sinners that God loves them."

"Well, he is wrong!"

"I think you will agree with him when you hear him because he backs up everything he says with the Word of God."

An inquisitive Moody went to hear the young preacher,

and he noticed that everyone was carrying a Bible, something strange to him. Again Moorehouse preached from John 3:16, and he gave chapter and verse references from Genesis to Revelation to prove that in all ages God loved the world.[7]

For seven nights the young man preached on John 3:16. "This heart of mine began to thaw out," Moody admitted. "I could not keep back the tears. It was like news from a far country; I just drank it in. So did the crowded congregation."[8]

To know the power of God's love, the more excellent way, became Moody's lifetime goal. Soon his ministry dramatically increased. "I used to preach that God was behind the sinner with a double-edged sword, ready to hew him down. I am through with that. I preach now that God is behind the sinner with love, and he is running away from the God of love."[9]

The Holy Spirit manifests Himself in the world chiefly as the love of God shining in and through individual Christian lives, Moody said. The Christian possesses joy (love exulting), peace (love in repose), long-suffering (love enduring), and goodness (love in action).[10]

Love was the key to Moody's theology and charisma; single-mindedness was the glue that held his exuberance in place.

SINGLE-MINDEDNESS

Moody often said,

The trouble with a great many men is that they spread themselves out over too much ground. They fail in everything. If they would only put their life into one channel, and keep it, they would accomplish something. They make no impression, because they do a little work here and little work there. . . . Lay yourselves on the altar of God, and then concentrate on some one work.[11]

Moody followed this philosophy throughout his life, beginning with his decision to leave a secular career to pursue God's work. Many milestones in his life can be attributed to a single-minded endeavor. For instance, in the winter of 1871, Moody focused his prayers on one desire: to know God more intimately. One day he was discussing his search with English evangelist Douglas Russell, when the preacher remarked, "Every believer is a child of God, being born of the Holy Spirit, but not every believer has received the filling of the Holy Spirit for service."[12]

Throughout the night and the next day, Moody was on his knees praying for this commission. He became conscious of a supernatural power controlling him:

> It is almost too sacred an experience to name. . . . I can only say God revealed to me, and I had such an experience of His love that I had to ask Him to stay His hand. . . . I went to preaching again. The sermons were not different, I did not present any new truths, and yet hundreds were converted. I would not now be placed back where I was before that blessed experience if you would give me all the world.[13]

"It is through the Holy Ghost that we get life," the evangelist later testified. "We would in reality not know Christ but for the Holy Ghost. . . . There is no life or power for a man to serve God until he is first born of the Spirit, until he has been quickened by the Holy Ghost, until he has been raised as Christ's dead body was raised."[14]

The next year, in 1872, Moody received the challenge from evangelist Henry Varley that I quoted at the beginning of this chapter: "The world has yet to see what God can do with and for and through and in a man who is fully consecrated to Him."

"By the Holy Spirit in me, I'll be that man," Moody vowed.[15] Once again, Moody made a single-minded decision that would change the course of his life. He "lost interest in everything except the preaching of Christ and working for souls."[16] Quickly, he broke the bonds of the busywork that encumbered him—the rebuilding of his church after the Great Chicago Fire and the construction of a new YMCA building—and left for England to begin again, this time as a traveling evangelist.

At first Moody's English trip seemed doomed. He arrived in England with singing evangelist Ira Sankey and their families only to learn that the men who had promised him financial support had died. Moody had only one other possibility: an invitation from the lay director of the YMCA in York to conduct meetings there, a suggestion he had ignored earlier. He descended upon York at the last minute, a hasty maneuver that crippled his efforts.

But Moody persevered. Despite the rocky start, he moved to Sunderland three weeks later, then for a short visit to the small town of Jarrow, and finally to Newcastle.

"Moody and Sankey entered Newcastle . . . almost as strangers in a strange land," observers admitted. "The general public knew no more about them than could be gathered from the bills on walls, which simply stated that Mr. Moody would 'preach' the gospel, and Mr. Sankey would 'sing' the gospel."[17]

But day after day, the preaching proved to be of God. Attendance began to pick up. Enthusiasm spread. Moody and Sankey moved from the edge of disaster to the brink of their illustrious careers as a revivalist and a gospel singer.

A minister of the Scottish Free Church heard of the stirrings of the Spirit in Newcastle and invited Moody to come to Scotland. For the next two years Moody and Sankey traveled from city to city. "Wherever they went they attracted huge crowds. At the meeting in Edinburgh, held in one the largest meeting places in the city, crowds 'densely packed'" every corner.'" '. . .'" a spokesman of the United Presbyterian Church asserted.[18]

As enthusiasm in England built, the variety and length of the reports in American newspapers mounted. According to one magazine article, "By the time the evangelist reached London he was already being approached informally about conducting services in New York, Chicago, and Philadelphia."[19] Moody's single-minded concentration on one channel—evangelism—led to excellence.

One of Moody's last utterances summed up the man as plainly as possible. "By and by you will hear people say, 'Mr. Moody is dead.' Don't you believe a word of it. At that very moment I shall be more alive than I am now. I shall then truly begin to live. I was born of the flesh in 1837. I was born of the Spirit in 1856. That which is born of the flesh may die. That which is born of the Spirit will live forever."[20]

D. L. Moody's "proclamation theology" lives today in a way he never imagined. Moody Bible Institute, which he began in 1886, trains thousands of students each year. The Moody radio station, begun in the early 1920s, owns and operates more than seventy stations, and it produces programs aired on more than 1,500 stations worldwide.

Moody dreamed of mass publishing Christian literature. This vision has become a reality through Moody Publishers. Originally founded by D. L. Moody in 1894 as the Bible Institute Colportage Association (BICA), Moody Publishers has distributed over 300 million books in its history.

Moody was not a man too different from most of us. He was not a scholar. He was not a theologian. He was not a man of eloquence. During his lifetime he grew from an impetuous, undirected young man to a man who was single-mindedly committed to serve the Lord. If God could take Moody with his limitations and enable him to excel, what can He do for you?

The Lord gets his best soldiers out of the highlands of affliction.

Charles H. Spurgeon

As sure as God puts his children into the furnace of affliction, He will be with them in it.

Charles H. Spurgeon

Expect great things from God; attempt great things for God.

Missionary William Carey

The Lord has laid me low, that I may look more simply to Him.

Missionary William Carey

NINETEENTH-CENTURY HEROES OF EXCELLENCE

And what does the LORD require of you?
To act justly and to love mercy and
to walk humbly with your God.

Micah 6:8 NIV

My Son, do not make light of the Lord's discipline,
and do not lose heart when he rebukes you,
because the Lord disciplines the one he loves.

Hebrews 12:5–6 NIV

After I studied D. L. Moody's life, I decided to compare two very different men, Charles Haddon Spurgeon, the famous British preacher, and William Carey, the father of modern missions. Spurgeon and Carey came from dissimilar backgrounds and were men of entirely different personalities. But both Spurgeon's and Carey's journeys to God had similarities, touch points that seem far from coincidental. Again I saw the clear marks of excellence: faith, character, action, perseverance, staying power, and suffering. I realized that they were not too different from any of us.

FAITH AND CHARACTER

Some dismiss Christianity as a way of life for themselves because they think that all God's people are born with an overwhelming bent to spirituality. As a result, they reject God's ability to reach them, since they know they are far from perfect. The excuse sounds rational to an atheist, but if you study great followers of God, you will find many of them began life as rebels. Certainly no one in the village of Paulersbury, England, where William Carey was born, would ever have expected him to become a missionary. Carey himself admitted he was a boisterous village lad, "addicted to swearing, lying and unchaste conversation." He described his companions as those who "could only serve to debase the mind, and lead me into the depths of that gross conduct which prevails among the lower classes in the most neglected villages."[1]

Carey's questionable character led him to commit an act that in those days verged on larceny. As a young apprentice shoemaker, he was delivering goods to an ironmonger when the man asked, "Would you prefer to have a sixpence or a shilling [for your Christmas tip]?"

The answer was obvious, "A shilling!"

After a few more calls, Carey had enough money to purchase some items he had long wanted, but the store owner rejected the silver shilling as counterfeit. Carey quickly substituted a shilling from the money he had collected for his employer, although his conscience told him that was wrong. If Carey had taken one pence more than that shilling, he would have been guilty of grand larceny, which was a capital offense at that time. Instead, he was severely reprimanded when his employer discovered the theft a few days later.[2]

Carey's conscience convicted him. He realized he was a sinner, and he was sure God did, too. On February 10, 1779, he decided to attend a service of intercession with the senior apprentice, John Warr, who was a Baptist. The preacher made a powerful appeal for complete commitment to Christ, and Carey was filled with repentance and a desire to know God, the first step on his journey to excellence. His questionable character was changed by God's salvation.

Charles Spurgeon was quite different. Few people would have thought Spurgeon needed to be convicted of sin. The Reverend Richard Hill had told Spurgeon's grandfather, "I do not know how it is, but I feel a solemn presentiment that this child will preach the Gospel to thousands, and God will bless him to many souls."[3]

Were Reverend Hill's words a self-fulfilling prophecy? Spurgeon later admitted, "I think so. I believed them, and looked forward to the time when I should preach the Word. I felt very powerfully that no unconverted person might dare to enter the ministry. This made me the more intent on seeking salvation, and more hopeful of it."[4]

The young boy's desire to serve God led him to realize how often he was tempted to sin.

I resolved that, in the town where I lived, I would visit every place of worship in order to find out the way of salvation. . . . At last one snowy day. . . . [I found] a Primitive Methodist's chapel. . . . A very thin-looking man came into the pulpit and opened his Bible and read these words; "Look unto me, and be ye saved, all the ends of the earth." Just setting his eyes upon me as if he knew me all by heart, he said: "Young man, you are in trouble." Well, I was, sure enough. Says he, "You will never get out of it unless you look to Christ," he said. And then, lifting up his hands, he cried out, as only, I think, a Primitive Methodist could do, "Look, look, look! It's only look!" said he. I saw at once the way of salvation.[5]

No matter how we experience it, no matter how small or large the evil we do might be, we must first be convicted of our sins. Charles Spurgeon never forgot that moment in his life or the need to have his sins forgiven; each of the sermons he preached had a special appeal to the unconverted. Spurgeon knew that each person must realize the evil within him and call out to God for salvation. Conversion is always preceded by conviction of sin and followed by faith in Christ.

ACTION

Once both men had committed their lives to the Lord, they quickly put their faith into action by serving small, rural churches that could not afford a minister. Because of his youth, Spurgeon saw himself as an assistant rather than the preacher, until on one assignment his companion made it clear that he could not and would not preach. There would be no sermon that day unless Spurgeon gave it. He recalled the events:

Praying for divine help, I resolved to make an attempt. . . . How long and how short it was I cannot now remember. It was not half such a task as I feared it would be, but I was glad to see my way to a fair conclusion and to the giving out of the last hymn. To my delight I had not broken down, nor stopped short in the middle, nor been destitute of ideas. . . .

I took up the book, but to my astonishment an aged voice cried out, "How old are you?"

"I am under sixty."

"Yes, and under sixteen," was the old lady's rejoinder.

"Never mind my age, think of the Lord Jesus and his preciousness," was all I could say, after promising to come again if the gentlemen at Cambridge thought me fit to do so.[6]

And, of course, they did. The young man preached every evening after school and he soon accepted his first pastorate at Waterbeach, a village near Cambridge. In the next few years, the church grew from forty members to one hundred.

Only three years after his conversion, William Carey was preaching regularly at Earls Barton Church, a tiny Dissenter congregation that relied on visiting lay preachers. The apprentice shoemaker had studied the commentaries and books of his employer and with the help of a friend even taught himself Greek. Carey soon began to question the church's reluctance to spread the gospel to foreign lands. He mentioned the subject at a fraternal meeting of ministers in 1786, but he was quickly reprimanded by the aged chairman of the meeting, who said, "You are a miserable enthusiast for asking such a question. Nothing can be done before another Pentecost."

Carey was mortified by the censure.

PERSEVERANCE AND STAYING POWER

But both Carey and Spurgeon persevered. Carey remained silent for the rest of that one meeting, but six years later he wrote a pamphlet, *An Enquiry into the Obligation of Christians to Use Means for the Conversion of the Heathens*, which refuted the five major arguments against missionary endeavors.

The distance of heathen lands, Carey said, was no longer a valid excuse. After all, since the invention of the compass, men could sail "with as much certainty through the great South Sea as they can through the Mediterranean."

The heathens' barbarous ways were no impediment to commercial men, Carey reminded the ministers. "It only requires that we should have as much love to the souls of our fellow-creatures . . . as they have for the profits arising for a few otter-skins."

Carey also dismissed the language barrier and the difficulty of procuring supplies. Again he reminded his fellow Christians that commercial men managed to communicate with other nations through interpreters. If this was not possible, missionaries could "mingle with the people till they have learned so much of their language as to be able to communicate." In the same way, missionaries could learn to grow the foods the natives ate.

Finally, Carey foresaw the modern practice of training indigenous missionaries to minister to their own people.

It might likewise be of importance . . . for them to encourage any appearance of gifts amongst the people of their charge; if such should be raised up, many advantages would be derived from their knowledge of the language, and customs of their countrymen; and their change of conduct would give great weight to their ministrations.[7]

Prophetic words! Words that Carey himself would soon live by. One might well dub his *Enquiry* the missionary manifesto.

Less than three weeks later, Carey preached the invitation sermon at the Baptist Association Meeting. "Enlarge the place of your tent," he exhorted, quoting Isaiah 54:2. "And let them stretch out the curtains of your habitations." He reprimanded the lifeless Anglican church and his own Baptist denomination for its lack of missionary vision and faith. "Expect great things from God. Attempt great things for God," he challenged. Have faith; anyone can achieve the impossible.

There was little reaction to Carey's sermon—either that day or the next morning at the business meeting. When the meeting was about to close without any consideration of the missionary issue, Carey again persevered. He turned to Andrew Fuller, a man of influence in Baptist circles, and asked, "Is nothing *again* going to be done?"

The direct appeal ignited Fuller's own conviction. He proposed "that a plan be prepared against the next Ministers' Meeting at Kettering, for forming a Baptist Society for propagating the Gospel among the Heathens."[8] Carey's perseverance called the Baptist Society into being. It would take the next twenty years to accomplish his vision. William Carey and his family went to India with John Thomas, a Baptist and former naval surgeon who had been a ship's doctor for the East India Company, and his family on June 13, 1793. For seven years they struggled to survive, learn the language, and communicate their faith to the natives. Their first major breakthrough occurred one morning in November of 1800 when a young Bengali carpenter, Krishna Pal, slipped on the steps to the Ganges and dislocated his right shoulder. Thomas had opened a clinic, since the villages had no access to doctors or medicines. He quickly set the bones and then took the opportunity to tell the Bengali carpenter how Christ could heal a man's soul as well as his shoulder. The next day, Carey visited the young man and suggested that he come to the mission for medicine to soothe the pain in his shoulder. After that, Krishna and a friend, Gokul, visited the mission regularly.

The superstitious Indians had difficulty understanding that Christ could die and yet live—and that because of this they, too, could become immortal. But Carey and Thomas persevered, patiently explaining God's redemptive love. By December 22, Krishna and Gokul affirmed their belief that Jesus died to save them, and they asked to be baptized.

Their joyful declaration of faith was seen by the mission servants as a renunciation of India; Krishna Pal and Gokul had become Europeans. On their way home that day, the young men were attacked. The continuing persecution caused Gokul's wife and mother to leave home, which forced him to disassociate himself from the Christians so that his family could be reunited. Only Krishna eventually was baptized in the Ganges on December 28. The young Indian carpenter later become the first native missionary to Calcutta and the first Bengali hymn writer.[9]

William Carey was known for his staying power. He once said to his nephew,

> Eustace, if after my removal any one should think it worth his while to write my Life, I will give you a criterion by which you may judge its correctness. If he give me credit for being a plodder, he will describe me justly. I can plod. I can persevere in any definite pursuit. To this I owe everything.[10]

Staying power, perseverance, and single-minded dedication to the Lord marked both Carey's and Spurgeon's lives. As I studied their histories, the comparison that surprised and blessed me most was how tragedy led to their most outstanding accomplishments.

SUFFERING

Carey's and Spurgeon's ministries were both marked by great disasters that would have defeated many of us. Carey did not see the fruits of his labor until the nineteenth century, almost twenty years after he arrived in India. By that time, he had completed a revision of the second Bengali version of the Bible, and he had also established a publishing company and free mission schools for low caste and orphaned children in Mudnabatti, Serampore, Calcutta, and Cutwa.

Then on the evening of March 11, 1812, a fire demolished the mission, all Carey's manuscripts, and all the Bible versions in the publishing company's warehouse. "In one short evening," Carey said as he walked through the smoking desolation the next day,

> the labours of years are consumed. How unsearchable are the ways of God! I had lately brought some things to the utmost perfection of which they seemed capable, and contemplated the missionary establishment with perhaps too much self-congratulation. The Lord has laid me low, that I may look more simply to him.[11]

Faith. Single-mindedness. Staying power. With God's grace and these attributes, Carey doggedly set to work to rewrite his translations, and God blessed his determination. A new and more efficient press rose from the old company. Because of reports about the fire, the work of the mission became known throughout Great Britain, and contributions flowed in from churches of all denominations.

> The greatest disaster of Carey's career led to his greatest successes.

"The fire has given your undertaking a celebrity which nothing else, it seems, could; a celebrity which makes me tremble. The public is not giving us their praises," wrote Andrew Fuller, the man who helped Carey begin the Baptist Missionary Society and who became its faithful secretary. The greatest disaster of Carey's career led to his greatest successes.

The same kind of overwhelming tragedy also threatened Charles Spurgeon's ministry. When Spurgeon assumed his second pastorate at the New Park Street Chapel, he found only one hundred people worshiping there. Instead of moving from church to church to achieve prominence, he restored the membership of the chapel to its earlier size—and even beyond, so that the building had to be renovated to accommodate the increasing membership. The congregation moved to Exeter Hall in the interim, one of the largest in London, and then to Surrey Gardens Music Hall as the crowds increased.

Disaster struck there on October 19, 1865. After the opening hymn and the Scripture had been read and discussed, Spurgeon stood up to lead the seven thousand people in prayer.

"Fire!" someone screamed, "Fire! Fire!" The call echoed throughout the hall, as others took up the alarm. People raced for every exit. Spurgeon implored the multitude to keep their seats, assuring them that there was no danger. The cry was a false alarm, but no one listened.

A reporter for *The Freeman* described the chaos:

Soon the hall and its staircases and passages presented a scene which baffles description. . . . Many, unable to reach the doors, wildly dashed through the windows, or leaped from the galleries to the floor, cutting and wounding themselves in their frenzied efforts. . . . The strong iron balustrade . . . gave way before the tremendous pressure, and a heap of persons were precipitated to the pavement below.[12]

Seven persons were killed, and not less than twenty-eight were seriously injured. Even more might have died if Spurgeon had not regained control and begun preaching at the request of those who remained.

My friends, there is a terrible day coming, when the terror and alarm of this evening shall be as nothing. That will be a time when the thunder and lighting and blackest darkness shall have their fullest power. . . .

The alarm which has just arisen has been produced, in some measure, by that instinct which teaches us to seek. . . . 'tis conscience that makes cowards of them. Many were afraid to stop here, because they thought it was to stop and be damned. They were aware—and many of you are aware—that if you were hurried before your Maker to-night, you would be brought there . . . unpardoned, and condemned. But what are your terrors now to what they will be on that terrible day of reckoning of the Almighty, when the heaven shall shrink above you, and hell open her mouth beneath you? . . .

Have you ever heard the welcome news that Jesus came into the world to save sinners? You are the chief among sinners. Believe that Christ died for you, and you may be saved from the torments of hell that await you.

In the midst of the confusion, Spurgeon preached the call to salvation he so believed in. Finally, he announced, "If our friends will go out by the central doors, we will sing while they go, and pray that some good may yet come out of this great evil after all."[13]

During the next days, Spurgeon was overcome with anguish and depression. But by the last Sunday in October, he was able to preach in the pulpit of the refurbished New Park Street Chapel. "Thy servant feared he should not have addressed this congregation again," he admitted. "But Thou hast brought him from the fiery furnace, and not even a smell of fire has passed upon him."[14]

Years later, Spurgeon admitted,

That frightful calamity, the impression of which can never be erased from my mind, turned out, in the providence of God, to be one of the most wonderful means of turning public attention to special services, and I do not doubt that, fearful catastrophe though it was, it has been the mother of multitudes of blessings.[15]

In the years following the disaster, the chapel was renovated three more times, and the congregation finally built the Metropolitan Tabernacle, which seated five thousand and provided standing room for one thousand.

As He had done with the patriarchs of old, God used the suffering in Spurgeon's life to achieve excellence. Spurgeon had faith. He persevered. Despite his lack of theological training, he became to England what D. L. Moody was to America, often speaking to crowds in excess of twenty thousand people. He, like Moody, founded numerous institutions: a college, an orphanage, almshouses for the poor, and a gospel literature publishing business. During his lifetime of fifty-seven years, more than thirty-five hundred of his sermons were published. He wrote 135 books and edited more than twenty-five others, even though he often felt that "writing is the work of a slave."[16]

Both Spurgeon and Carey steadfastly held to their faith in God during moments of disaster. And God blessed their suffering. When disaster strikes your life, don't think as Job did—and as we tend to think: *I will never be happy again.* Instead, wait with awe to see how God will use your tragedy to His glory.

Spurgeon summed up his life on his deathbed. He whispered to his wife, "Oh, wife, I have had such a blessed time with my Lord."[17] The great preacher's walk through this world led to excellence because it was taken hand in hand with a God who stood at his shoulder guiding him on. Spurgeon was never alone, and we are never alone!

As he was dying, Carey witnessed, too, to a friend who had inspired him in the course of his life. A Scottish missionary, Alexander Duff, reminded Carey of his notable achievements.

"Mr. Duff," Carey whispered to him, "you have been speaking about Dr. Carey, Dr. Carey; when I am gone, say nothing about Dr. Carey—speak about Dr. Carey's Savior."[18]

Both Spurgeon and Carey finished their lives giving glory to the same Savior, who had taken the entirely different natures of two men from entirely different backgrounds and had led them to achieve excellence. The environmentalists argue that environment molds a person's character. The behaviorists argue that behavior makes the difference. I argue for Jesus who makes the eternal difference!

Neither Carey nor Spurgeon began life as saints. Both lived their lives as Christians under construction. Both walked humbly with their God as the prophet Micah requested. Only God can take our fallen natures and mold them into His image. Only God can lead men, women, and children to experience true excellence.

Some months before John Stott died, a friend was telling me about a final visit with him. By this time Dr. Stott had given up international travel. He had already preached his last sermon. He had written his last book. His health was progressively failing. He was clearly in the somber season. He used a walker. His sight was going. Ministrokes had destroyed his ability to do things.

He kept meeting with people and even took some calls, advising the Lausanne Committee and the Langham Partnership. But even that was winding down. His mind was still very active, but he was not able to lift his head and was slumped over, having a hard time holding himself up. Can you imagine a person of such influence being reduced to that—imprisoned by his own body? Yet in this visit, the man reported, Dr. Stott said, "Read 2 Corinthians 4 and 5 to me!" So the friend read these words:

> Therefore we do not lose heart. Though outwardly we are wasting away, yet inwardly we are being renewed day by day. For our light and momentary troubles are achieving for us an eternal glory that far outweighs them all. So we fix our eyes not on what is seen, but on what is unseen. For what is seen is temporary, but what is unseen is eternal. . . .

Donald W. Sweeting and George Sweeting, *How to Finish the Christian Life*

PRESENT-DAY HEROES OF EXCELLENCE

"Those who are wise will shine like the brightness
of the heavens, and those who lead many
to righteousness, like the stars forever and ever."

Daniel 12:3 NIV

And whatever you do, whether in word or deed,
do it all in the name of the Lord Jesus, giving
thanks to God the Father through Him.

Colossians 3:17 NIV

We are all familiar with the parable of the talents. The servant who received five talents increased them to ten. The second servant received two talents and doubled them. And the fearful servant took his one talent and buried it.

Seeking security in this world is natural. We are inclined to save our money under our beds or in safety deposit boxes. We are also inclined to save our talents. But God is not calling us to follow our inclinations. He calls us to excel. No one doubts who excelled in this parable. Two of the servants heard their master say, "Well done, good and faithful servant; you were faithful over a few things, I will make you ruler over many things. Enter into the joy of your lord" (Matt. 25:21).

The third servant was thrown into darkness, and all that had been given him was taken away. In our fallen world, being like the third servant is all too easy. But notice, two of the three servants overcame their natural instincts. They excelled!

Excellence, as I said before, is not only for a chosen few. It is for each of us if we commit ourselves to follow Jesus.

Moody, Spurgeon, and Carey were ministers, but thousands of others serve Christ with the fruits of their labors—their money—and the gifts of talents.

Here are four, twentieth-century followers of Jesus, who reflect the same marks of excellence that we've seen in the lives of Moody, Spurgeon, and others. Henry P. Crowell, founder of the Quaker Oats Company; his son, Henry Coleman Crowell, Yale graduate, engineer, and creative leader at Moody Bible Institute for forty years; John E. Haggai, MBI graduate, prolific writer, pastor, evangelist, and innovative missionary leader; and Joni Erickson Tada, gifted author and compassionate spokesperson for all who suffer. Put yourself in their shoes as I trace their journeys to excellence.

HENRY PARSONS CROWELL

Remember how you felt at age nine? Just beginning to make your own friends, to search for your own identity—hopefully with the support and guidance of a loving mother and father. At that time of his life, Henry Parsons Crowell stood at his father's graveside. We can imagine how lost and bewildered he felt.

After the minister spoke the final words of committal,

Henry Parsons Crowell asked to talk with him about some disturbing questions, questions about death—and life. The boy was seeking strength to continue without his father's loving support. The next day the two knelt in the minister's study as the boy gave his life to the Lord, asking Him to guide him as his father had.[1]

This father/son relationship deepened when seventeen-year-old Henry was stricken with consumption, the disease that killed his father, and was told to quit school and give up his plans to attend college. The ghost he must have feared at his father's graveside had come to haunt him. For two years he rested and worked as a part-time shoe salesman in the firm his father had established. During that time, he heard D. L. Moody repeat Henry Varley's words: "The world has yet to see what God can do with and for and through and in a man who is fully and wholly consecrated to Him."

"Varley meant *any* man," Moody testified at the meeting. "Varley didn't say he had to be educated, or brilliant, or anything else! Just, *a man!* Well, with the Holy Spirit in me, I'll be *one* of those men!"

Moody's words deeply affected young Crowell:

I saw now that the wrecking of my school plans didn't really matter. God didn't need his men educated, or brilliant, or anything else! All God needed was just a man! Well by the grace of God, I would be God's man! To be sure, I would never preach like Moody. But I could make money and help support the labors of people like Moody. Then I resolved, "Oh God, if You will allow me to make money to be used in Your service I will keep my name out of it so You will have the glory."[2]

That day Crowell turned his love for God into a commitment that lasted a lifetime, but his health continued to deteriorate, and in August of 1874, he was told to quit his job and do nothing but rest. Crowell's study of the Scriptures, which had begun in earnest when he first became sick, intensified. He became fascinated by the Bible's frequent reference to the number seven. One night he read a passage in the book of Job: "He shall deliver you in six troubles, yes, in seven no evil shall touch you" (5:19).

He believed God was speaking directly to him, telling him that he would not die at an early age. He believed this even when his condition became so critical that the doctors reevaluated his case and made a surprising recommendation: "Harry Crowell has to live out-of-doors the next seven years! or else!"[3]

To many young men this would have sounded like a life sentence; there was no promise of recovery, just an ultimatum. Seven years of resting while his friends went to college and began their careers. Yet Crowell saw the hand of God in the midst of the doctor's morbid predictions. The Lord would heal him after seven years outdoors.

Crowell went west to explore its beautiful terrain. He often felt lonely, especially when his fiancé's mother, believing he was terminally ill, forced her to cancel her engagement to him. Crowell could've literally "lain down and died," as the woman predicted, but it wasn't God's will for him, he knew. Crowell had faith, and slowly began to feel better. By the fourth year, he began to use the intelligence God had given him to buy and sell farmland in South Dakota. During the seventh and last year of his exile, a dry spell shriveled his wheat crop from twenty-five bushels per acre to eleven.

Is God moving me from farming? Crowell wondered. Within days, a man offered to buy his seventeen thousand acres and his valuable Percherons, which were excellent draft horses. Crowell sold the property and returned to Cleveland. "I felt that I was now in good health again, but I would just wait a while and see what God would do next. I knew He would show me what He wanted."[4]

And He did. Within thirty days of the sale, a man offered to sell Crowell a Quaker's mill at Ravenna. "I doubt if it will make a success," the man admitted.[5] But Crowell thought differently. Again he saw the hand of God. In his last seven years, he had learned to rely totally on His guidance.

Oats were traditionally fed to horses until Americans began to realize the grain's nutritional value. All that was needed to make the cereal a favorite of the American breakfast table was a man with marketing and organizational know-how, a man dedicated to excellence. Henry Parsons Crowell was that man. As early as 1882, he outlined his plan:

My policy has been to make better oatmeal and cereal of all kinds than has ever been manufactured; to combine such companies as are interested, and willing, into a chartered company with capital stock, having full control over all its units. This chartered company will scrap machinery, or even the mills of constituent members as improvement necessitates. The general company should displace old names with a single trade name, and seek a world market. To this end, it must do educational work, and create an oat demand where none existed. It is only by such a broad distribution and central management that we can avoid the perils of panic, competition, or disaster to some one plant or other.[6]

His plan was visionary—so innovative that it took Crowell twenty-five years to convince the small mill owners to give up their petty rivalries and organize the Quaker Oats Company. They were twenty-five years of patient waiting and relentless but gentle determination, but Crowell knew how to continue in faith when all seemed lost. He had developed single-mindedness and staying power.

If Crowell had died at forty-two, instead of at eighty-nine, he would have been known as an excellent Christian businessman. Once his fortune was established, he became a "business-priest," as Crowell defined it: "a man who acted on the idea that a man's business is not chiefly his way of making a living, but his altar where he serves the King."[7] His stewardship focused on three areas: his time, his money, and his social action. For more than forty years, he gave 65 percent of his income and a great deal of his time to God.

He adopted the fledgling Moody Bible Institute. The difference he made is described by P. B. Fitzwater, assistant to President James M. Gray: "Without Mr. Crowell, [there would be] nothing!"[8] Fitzwater watched Crowell handle many controversial issues throughout those years, guiding the Institute into a continually improving position of educational excellence and financial stability.

No one knows how much money Henry Crowell gave to Moody, since he was always fearful he would discourage other givers if the size of his gifts were known. Crowell wanted the Institute to be built by the gifts of many friends and not be dependent upon one giver.

When Will H. Houghton, Gray's successor, wanted to recognize Crowell's contributions by naming a new building after him, Crowell refused. "Years ago, I told the Lord that if He would allow me to make money for His service, I would keep my name out of it, so He could have the glory."

Instead, a blank space was left under the words *Moody Bible Institute* on the arch of the building. After Crowell's death, the words *Crowell Hall* were carved there.

Successful businessman. Christian leader. Business-priest. Advocate of decency and justice. The vow Crowell made in 1874 lasted for seventy years until his death in 1944. Talk about staying power! Henry Parsons Crowell was a man of God and a man committed to excellence. He took the talents God gave him and multiplied them a hundredfold.

HENRY COLEMAN CROWELL

Like his father, Henry Coleman Crowell was a person of excellence.

Richard E. Day gives us a snapshot of Coleman Crowell's college days and his dedication to the Moody Bible Institute.

Coleman matriculated in Yale 1917, and in his second year transferred to the Scheffield Scientific School. He graduated from Yale, June, 1921, with the degree Ph. B. Today he is Vice President of Moody Bible Institute, "thereby succeeding in what he esteems his father's chief work." In particular it is Mr. Crowell's interest to direct and coordinate the work of the three branches of the Institute. Tom Smith of the Moody Board writes: "I thank God for Henry Parsons Crowell's son, Coleman." He might well have added, "And I thank God for Susan Crowell, who in a peculiar way dedicated her son to this work."[9]

Henry Parsons Crowell's first wife was Lillie Augusta Wick, who was a joy and inspiration to him during his difficult years of physical illness. They married June 29, 1882.

Their marriage was blessed with a daughter, Annie Bayard Crowell on May 3, 1883. Following a brief illness, which resulted in great sorrow, Lillie passed away June 10, 1885.[10]

Several years later, Henry P. Crowell married Susan Coffin Coleman. Crowell's biographer states that Lillie was like "the morning star for his young manhood, inspiring him in his fight for health, and in his early business success. And Susan Coffin Coleman, with equal significance, blessed his mature years."[11] They were married July 10, 1888.

It is not possible to fully convey the contribution of the Crowell family to the Moody Bible Institute. The presence and guidance of this father-son duo included over eighty-two years of sacrificial ministry, preparing, protecting, and providing for the Moody Bible Institute.

Having been a student at Moody (1942–1945), I met and witnessed their loving care. I was privileged to meet both of them. It was not that I knew them as a close friend, but I knew them as admired and respected role models. They both reflected everyday excellence.

Gene Getz, in his book *The Story of Moody Bible Institute*, writes about Coleman Crowell's efforts to secure and establish Moody Radio. Getz writes, "The man who played, by far the most important role was young Henry Coleman Crowell." Getz continues, telling how Coleman "was transferred . . . to become assistant to the president [of MBI], where he was given the responsibility to oversee the development of the radio's work."[2]

Dr. Getz provides twenty pages detailing the challenges that faced Coleman Crowell, including the many trips to Washington, DC, to meet with the Federal Communicators Commission, answering their questions and meeting their requirements. The ministry of Moody Radio, over these many years, is a witness to the efforts and giftedness of Coleman Crowell. His life displayed character, faith, single-mindedness, and great perseverance.

Coleman Crowell's contributions were many during his forty years of service. His scientific skills welcomed Dr. Erwin Moon, and the possibilities of Moody Institute of Science. This ministry alone reached millions with the gospel around the world.

It was also Coleman Crowell who listened to the Moody alumni and the burdens of Larry Pearson (1946–1950) and Herbert Lockyer Jr. to update the alumni constitution and prepare a program enlisting Moody Alumni groups wherever possible. They also launched the Moody Alumni fund, which contributes significantly to the school yearly.

Coleman Crowell welcomed Moody Aviation and the possibility of its worldwide impact. Again, Dr. Getz tells how Henry Coleman Crowell quickly embraced the enormous possibilities of the ministry.

> In February 1946, [Paul] Robinson talked with institute leaders regarding a proposed plan which he had written up for training missionaries in aviation. Henry Coleman Crowell, executive vice-president of the institute, who had been the key man in the development of the radio ministry and the main promoter for Moody Institute of Science, took a vital interest in Robinson's proposal. Consequently Robinson received an invitation several weeks later to survey the Chicago area as a likely place to set up such a program.[13]

Moody Aviation has been a reality for over seventy years, reaching remote areas of the world with the saving gospel of Christ, as well as meeting the emergency needs of missionary families and the people they serve.

Coleman and his wife, Perry, served with a single heart. They are unforgettable heroes of excellence.

JOHN EDMUND HAGGAI

A third present-day hero of excellence is John Edmund Haggai.

It was September 1942 that I first met John Haggai. We were both entering freshmen at Chicago's Moody Bible Institute.

John arrived from Massachusetts, and I from New Jersey.

John's parents, Mildred and Waddy, also were students at Moody in 1913. They met while carrying out their practical Christian work assignment. This led to their courtship and eventual marriage in 1923.

Not only did John become a special friend, but so did John's parents, as I was invited to minister several times in the churches they pastored, leading a week-long evangelistic series.

John's mother, Mildred, traced her roots from England to New England in the 1650s. John's father, Waddy Haggai, was born in Damascus, Syria. He was won to the Christian faith through the witness of an uncle, who in turn was led to Christ through a book salesman, who had been led to the Lord by Presbyterian missionaries.

Life was dangerous for Syrian Christians, causing John's father and two brothers to flee for their lives to America.

In America, they lived with relatives who had preceded them to the US. After a few years, John's father enrolled as a student of the Moody Bible Institute.

Not only did John's father meet his life's partner at Moody, but so did John Haggai. Courtship and eventual marriage occurred often enough for students to jestfully refer to the school as "Moody Bridal Institute."

I actually met John Haggai's future wife while leading an evangelistic series at the Euclid Avenue Baptist Church in Bristol, Virginia, in 1943. Little did I imagine that the lovely, talented Christine Barker would meet and marry John and serve the Lord for over seventy-five years together.

John Edmund Haggai has always been a man of action. John graduated from Moody on August 2, 1945, was ordained the next day, August 3, and married August 4, 1945. I was there and served as his best man.

John was a young man in a hurry to give his best to the work of the Lord.

Following graduation from Moody, John and Christine headed south to pastor in Jackson Mills, South Carolina. Later they served in Lancaster, South Carolina, then Chattanooga, Tennessee, and Louisville, Kentucky. While in South Carolina, John furthered his education and graduated from Furman University.

John experienced such success in his pastorates that soon he was recognized as a gifted pastor, teacher, and evangelist and could have given his life to an itinerant ministry.

John and Christine often talked and prayed about beginning a family. It wasn't long after that, Christine became pregnant and experienced nine months of normal pregnancy. Little did they know what was before them.

On the night of Christine's delivery, their doctor, who was a specialist, was nowhere to be found. John tried in every way to reach him, but was unsuccessful. Let me share John's own words: "I got through to the specialist. Unbelievably, he was at a cocktail party." When he finally arrived, John writes, "I could tell he had been drinking." The result of the doctor's delay and inept delivery caused the baby to hemorrhage, "causing extensive brain damage. His jaw was badly injured. Both collarbones were broken. His right leg was pulled apart at the growing center."

John wrote, "I bowed my head . . . I know only that, I dared to believe that my Lord was sovereign in the valley as well as on the mountaintop."[14]

Johnny lived for twenty years, receiving extensive daily care, along with many weeks in emergency care. Yet, through it all, John and Christine Haggai passionately loved Johnny and accepted their trials as a gift of God.

From childhood, John E. Haggai possessed a serious sense of call to the work of world missions. As a preacher's kid, he sat under the teaching of his missions-minded father and the missionaries who regularly visited their church. John's call to missions resulted in the formation of Haggai Institute, now called Haggai International and celebrating fifty years of missionary service. The purpose of Haggai International is "to equip Asian, African and Latin American Christian leaders—who will train others—to reach their own people for Christ."[15] Only eternity will reveal all that God has done.

John and Christine have been beloved and admired friends of ours for over seventy-six years. Though separated by a thousand miles, rarely a week passes without communication.

Along with a multitude of friends worldwide, we salute them as present-day heroes of excellence.

Henry Parsons Crowell, Henry Coleman Crowell, and John Edmund Haggai are three of the many twentieth-century heroes of excellence. They used the talents God gave them and minimized their handicaps to give God the glory. They persevered!

The same could be said about women of excellence. History, as well as the present, abounds with gifted, committed, God-blessed women who are making an eternal difference.

WOMEN OF EXCELLENCE

The Bible records many women who excelled, like Eve, Jochebed, Miriam, Deborah, Ruth, Hannah, Esther, Elizabeth, and Mary, the mother of Jesus, just to mention a few.

The women mentioned in the life of the early church, as written in the New Testament, were impressive. For example, women were the very last to leave the place of the cross after Jesus was crucified (Mark 15:40–41), and women were the first to arrive at Jesus' tomb on Resurrection morning (John 20:1). And they were the first to announce Jesus' resurrection (Matt. 28:1–8). Women also attended the prayer meeting recorded in Acts 1:14, and they were among the first to welcome Paul and Silas as missionaries (Acts 16:13–15).

Only eternity will reveal the supernatural difference women have made over the centuries and in our present day.

Just think of the thousands of Bible studies conducted each day in homes, churches, and places of business. Though the men lead many, the preponderance is the work of godly, gifted women. It would not surprise me at all if God would bring to our world a spiritual awakening through gifted women, faithfully teaching the Bible.

I started to list the names of gifted women but soon realized there are so many that I would have to omit some, and chose not to do so. Though the list is large and significant, I will just speak briefly of one present-day woman who is a hero of excellence.

JONI EARECKSON TADA

I first met Joni in the early 1970s while I served as the president of Chicago's Moody Bible Institute. I had read about her horrific diving accident of July 30, 1967, in Maryland's Chesapeake Bay. Joni's family were followers of Christ and worshiped at the Reformed Episcopal Church of Catonsville, Maryland. Joni also enjoyed the ministry of Young Life clubs during her high school years. She excelled riding horses and playing tennis, hockey, and lacrosse. All that she enjoyed was suddenly taken from her. Because of this accident, Joni eventually was told that she would never walk again. That her injury was permanent.

Joni spent three and a half months in the hospital and then was moved to a center for rehabilitation, where she could learn how to live with her paralysis. After a while, Joni learned to draw and paint by holding the pencil or paintbrush in her teeth. Joni then went to another center where she learned to use a wheelchair and was fitted for arm braces. Then she learned how to use a spoon and her arms. Finally, she could leave the center and went to be with her sister, Jay. She struggled and couldn't understand why her prayers for healing were not answered.

Around this time, Joni began receiving invitations to give her testimony to various groups. She came to the Moody Bible Institute for our Founder's Week on a Saturday night in the 1970s. Joni's testimony was life-changing.

Before she spoke, she turned to me and asked, "Dr. S, would you adjust my wrist watch, so I can finish on time?" Joni couldn't even turn her wrist or wipe away a tear or scratch an itch.

God spoke in a supernatural way that Saturday night, and

hundreds in the audience decided to follow Jesus Christ—regardless of life's trials.

Amid Joni's pain and limitations, she has served sacrificially. Her book *Joni* is a classic.[16] A movie of her life was produced. An organization, "Joni and Friends," encourages disabled people. Joni also met a gifted teacher named Ken Tada, and they married and are a very special team.

Both Joni and Ken are to many of us heroes of present-day excellence, dedicated to God's glory.

Excellence isn't limited to biblical patriarchs or historical figures like Spurgeon and Carey or Joni and Ken Tada. It's available to each of us today. Instead of wondering why God gave you only three talents and your neighbor five, concentrate on how you and God can multiply your talents to His glory. That's the attitude that leads to excellence. It was the secret of Caleb and the patriarchs, of Moody, Spurgeon, Henry Parsons Crowell, Henry Coleman Crowell, John Edmund Haggai, and Joni and Ken Tada.

If I've learned anything in the study of noteworthy people, it is that no one is perfectly gifted. Also, no one is without handicaps. God takes ordinary men and women, like you and me, and through the power of His Holy Spirit enables them to excel for His glory.

Are you multiplying your talents? God is calling you to excel. He wishes to greet you in heaven with the same words He spoke to the two faithful servants, "Well done, good and faithful servant; you were faithful over a few things, I will make you ruler over many things. Enter into the joy of your lord" (Matt. 25:21).

We finish well by the grace of God. That is also how we start the race. That is what keeps us in the race. And that is what takes us to the end. As John Newton put it in his famous hymn, "'Tis grace hath brought me safe thus far, and grace will lead me home."

When all is said and done, grace is the ultimate explanation for why any of us make it.

Donald W. Sweeting and George Sweeting, *How to Finish the Christian Life*

THE ULTIMATE SECRET OF EXCELLENCE

"Dear friends, now we are children of God, and what we will
be has not yet been made known. But we know that when Christ
appears, we shall be like him, for we shall see him as he is."

1 John 3:2 NIV

"Not that I have already obtained all this, or have already
arrived at my goal, but I press on to take hold of that
for which Christ Jesus took hold of me."

Philippians 3:12 NIV

Keep on . . . keeping on!

For the most part, these are trying times to be alive. We have pros and cons, of course. Some people see a brightening in the economic picture, and others are pessimistic. Still others fear violence at home and abroad. They point to political unrest that afflicts our world. In the final analysis, only the coming years will tell the true tale of our times.

But good times or bad times only provide the backdrop for our own responses to the opportunities and challenges of life. Whether the year is a good one or a bad one depends on our responses to the opportunities that face us.

Everyone needs at least three ingredients for a successful

> Good times or bad times only provide the backdrop for our own responses to the opportunities and challenges of life.

life: (1) a self fit *to live with*, (2) a faith fit *to live by*, and (3) a work fit *to live for*. Do those three things apply to you?

First, do you have a self fit to live with? Or are you living with a self that makes each day a losing battle? The issue here is your personal faith in Jesus Christ. If you need a self fit *to* live with, the answer is found in Him. Jesus majors in changing lives for now and for all eternity.

Second, do you have a faith fit to live by? If you are a Christian, you should be building a faith to live by. Many people begin the Christian life only to get on a detour or fall by the wayside. Keep going! Become a student of the Bible and live it out each day. Pray. Tell others about your faith. Find a strong church and make it yours. Then you will enjoy an exciting, dynamic, vital faith—a faith fit to live by.

The third requirement is the one I want to emphasize. You need a work fit to live for. Do you have an inner calling that motivates you? Eating, sleeping, and making payments on a house are not enough. Even enjoying your work, getting ahead, and building a reputation will never satisfy. You hitch your wagon to a star only when you discover a work worth all you can give it. Paul's letter to the Philippians was written from the confines of a Roman jail, but it blazes with optimism and joy because he had a work fit to live for.

Listen to the apostle Paul's words recorded in Philippians

1:12: "But I want you to know, brethren, that the things which happened to me have actually turned out for the furtherance of the gospel." A little later Paul stated his ultimate goal: "That in nothing I shall be ashamed, but with all boldness, as always, so now also Christ will be magnified in my body, whether by life or by death" (v. 20).

Can you live at that level? Yes, you can. This is the way, above all others, to pursue biblical excellence.

Jesus challenged individuals with two simple, yet profound, life-changing words: "Follow Me" (Matt 4:19). Matthew, Andrew, Peter, James, John, and others like them left everything, rose up, and followed Him. Following Him would appear to be a simple act. Yet contained in these words is the ultimate secret of how to live a God-honoring life.

Jesus knew how to live. He never came to the close of a day and had to turn over a new leaf. On one occasion, He asked His accusers, "Which of you convicts Me of sin?" (John 8:46). He is the eternal Lamb without any blemish or spot. His desire has always been to do the will of God. Single-mindedly and steadfastly He set His face toward the cross. Even in His suffering, He prayed for those who crucified Him, "Father, forgive them; for they know not what they do" (Luke 23:34 KJV), In short, Jesus is not only the Savior for us sinners but also our ultimate

> **Jesus is not only the Savior for us sinners but also our ultimate role model. Christian excellence is Christlikeness!**

role model. Christian excellence is Christlikeness!

What does it mean to follow Jesus? Does Jesus still ask men and women to follow Him today? Yes, He does. To follow Jesus means to make Him first in your life. It means putting aside your personal program and getting involved in His program.

That is exactly what the disciples did. Andrew, Peter, James, and John were in the fishing business, but when Jesus called them, they left it all behind. Matthew had probably worked for years to gain his position as a tax collector, but when Jesus came along, he made a choice. He left his table and his title and followed Jesus.

The point is not that they changed their occupations. No, the point is that they switched from serving themselves to serving Jesus. They took up service in an infinitely greater cause.

Have you done that? If your life seems hardly worth the trouble, it may be because you've never found your larger job. Even though you're a professing Christian, you've never really followed Jesus.

How can you follow Him? First, you'll have to volunteer. Jesus said, "If anyone desires to come after Me, let him deny himself, and take up his cross daily, and follow Me" (Luke 9:23). The gospel writers have told us that Jesus was speaking not only to the disciples but also to a larger group of less committed people. Wherever you are in your spiritual journey, you can say yes or no to the call to follow Him. If you are unconverted, you will have to take this first step. You will have to let Jesus Christ do something for you, before He can work through you.

Many people who have received Christ as their Savior seem to stop at that point. Their lives are crowded with their own interests. They have no time or strength for God. No wonder they fail to excel. This brings us to the second step: you'll have to pay a price.

Remember what Jesus said about taking up the cross daily and following Him. A cross is not pleasant. It's designed for executions. We all know some people who speak of the burdens they have to bear as "their crosses." Of course, Christians have problems. We have sicknesses and sorrows. We face tough times. We have burdens and frustrations. But Jesus was referring to something else in this passage. He was saying that if we want to follow Him, we must give up our right to live for ourselves each day of our lives.

Years ago I discovered something. Maybe you have learned it, too. I cannot serve myself and also serve the Lord. If I try to impress others with George Sweeting, I can't do much for God. Only as I forget myself and get wrapped up in serving Jesus and others does anything happen that really counts.

Self has always been Public Enemy Number One to Christian maturity. The apostle Paul grieved that there was no one in Philippi to minister to the church there, "For I have no one like-minded," he said, "who will sincerely care for your state." Then he added the sad statement, "For all seek their own, not the things which are of Christ Jesus" (Phil. 2:20–21). Therefore, he sent Timothy to remind them of their calling.

Here's a test for you. Whose interests are you looking out for? Yours—or Jesus Christ's? Remember, Jesus said, "If you want to follow Me, go out and bury your own self-interest and get wrapped up in My interests."

How then do you become a follower of Jesus? First, you

must volunteer. Second, you must lay aside your personal program and give yourself to His plan. Finally, you will have to follow in His footsteps.

Jesus chose His words carefully. He was telling each of us to follow a leader and become a companion. He was teaching us to adopt the idea of union, of likeness—individually traveling the same course.

We should be like Jesus in many ways. Like Him, we should seek the glory of God the Father. Like Him, we should be supremely concerned about lost souls. "For the Son of Man has come to save that which was lost" (Matt. 18:11).

Of course, we cannot offer our lives as Jesus did, but we can lay down our lives that others might know Him. Often this means killing our natural desires to respond in anger to anger, to return hatred with hatred, and to wish evil on those who ensnare us.

Jesus' purpose in life was to carry out the will of His Father. "I have food to eat of which you do not know," He told the disciples (John 4:32). And then He explained, "My food is to do the will of Him who sent Me, and to finish His work" (John 4:34).

Is it your purpose to do God's will and finish His work?

Kenneth Wuest was for many years a gifted and beloved teacher of Greek at Moody Bible Institute. He translated Luke 9:23 this way: "Assuming that anyone desires to come after me as a follower of mine, let him disregard his own interests and let him at once—and once for all—pick up and carry his cross day after day. . . . Let him take the same road with me that I take as a habit of life."

That is the essence of following Jesus. It's not a matter of occupation. It's where your heart is, where your interests lie. It's how you spend your strength.

A great man of God in D. L. Moody's day owned a meat-packing company. When people asked his occupation, he would often answer, "I serve the Lord, but I pack pork to pay expenses." Some of the greatest followers of Christ I know have had other occupations to pay expenses. They have been boat builders, bankers, truckers, farmers, sales representatives, teachers—the list goes on and on. Their employment is not really important, but who and what comes first is what really matters.

Are you following Jesus? Are His purposes your primary concern? Or have you tried to save yourself and filled your life with your own program? You can tell by how you pray and give and work. If all you do points to your own wants and needs, you are probably not following Christ.

Since the earliest days of the Christian church, no one has failed by following Jesus. Listen to the words of Luke 18:29-30: "There is no one who has left house or parents or brothers or wife or children, for the sake of the kingdom of God, who shall not receive many times more in this present time, and in the age to come eternal life."

It pays in the long run (and short run) to follow the Lord. In fact, the future is as bright as the promises of God. A day is coming when each believer will be literally like Christ. At that time, each of us will experience complete and ultimate excellence.

It also pays to follow Christ here and now. John 12:26 contains two thrilling promises. The first is this: "If anyone serves Me, let him follow Me; and where I am, there My servant will be also." Are these words speaking of the future? Of life after death? Perhaps in part, but I am sure there is something more in this passage. Jesus is in the world today, working through the Holy Spirit. The man or woman who follows Him will know His continual presence. Oh, the thrill and the strength of God's constant presence day after day.

The second promise of this verse is, "If anyone serves Me, him My Father will honor." Did you hear that? Across this nation and around the world I see the mighty hand of God honoring and lifting up those men and women who are truly following Jesus. God is doing marvelous things in their lives. God is blessing them. These followers would not trade places with kings, emperors, millionaires, tycoons, or those who names appear in the bright lights. They know the inspiring presence of God Himself as they press forward and upward "toward the goal for the prize of the upward call of God in Christ Jesus" (Phil. 3:14).

Following Jesus is costly but eternally rewarding. It gets better each day and every year. The best is yet to come. I could have no better wish for you than that you experience the joy and thrill of following Him, because Jesus Christ is the ultimate embodiment and reality of excellence.

ACKNOWLEDGMENTS

My words cannot adequately convey my heartfelt gratitude to all who serve at Moody Publishers.

I began writing for Moody in 1971 when, by God's grace, I became the sixth president of Moody Bible Institute.

Our founder, D. L. Moody, had a passion for the printed page. He poured his life into providing the message of salvation and spiritual growth for all to read. World evangelization was his mission. He spoke to millions in person and multiplied millions through books.

The Moody Publishers team are the heirs of D. L. Moody today.

Personally, I express my gratitude for the guidance of Greg Thornton, Paul Santhouse, Randall Payleitner, and Connor Sterchi. Together we share, to the glory of God (Ps. 115:1).

NOTES

Chapter 1: The Challenge to Excellence

1. Donna Nelson, "America's Compassionate Chief Physician," *The Saturday Evening Post*, May/June 1982, 16.

2. Taken from an English translation of the Oath of Hippocrates, which goes back more than two thousand years. In recent years, the Declaration of Geneva, adopted in September 1948 by the General Assembly of the World Medical Organization and modeled closely on the Hippocratic Oath, has been used by more and more medical schools.

3. C. Everett Koop, *The Right to Live: The Right to Die* (Wheaton, IL: Tyndale, 1976), 27.

4. Ibid.

5. First International Conference on Abortion, Fall of 1967, Washington, D.C.. Sponsored by Harvard Divinity School and Joseph P. Kennedy, Jr., Foundation; quoted in Koop, *The Right to Live*, 47.

6. John W. Gardner, *Excellence* (New York: Harper & Row, 1961), 86.

7. George Eliot, *Scenes of Clerical Life,* (1857; repr., London: Penguin Classics, 1998), 47.

8. "mediocre," Dictionary.com, based on the Random House Unabridged Dictionary, © Random House, Inc. 2019, https://www.dictionary.com/browse/mediocre.

9. Charles Close, *Excellence: The Pursuit, the Commitment, the Achievement* (Dallas: L.T.V., 1981), 44.

Chapter 2: Faith—The Power to Move Mountains

1. The LTV Corporation Washington Seminar, 1981, 30.

Chapter 3: Character—The Purity to Serve

1. *Encyclopedia Britannica* (Chicago: Encyclopedia Britannica Co., 1984), s.v. "Burr, Aaron."

2. William Barclay, *Letters to the Galatians and Ephesians* (Philadelphia; Westminster, 1976), 100.

3. Batsell Barrett Baxter, *America, It's Not Too Late* (Grand Rapids: Baker, 1974), 79.

4. Franklin K. Lane, *The Making of Herbert Hoover* (New York: Century, 1920), 333.

5. J. R. Miller, *The Building of Character* (New York: Thomas Y. Crowell, 1975), 6.

Chapter 4: Action—The Commitment to Make a Difference

1. George H. Fox, *Survivor Number Three* (Whittier, CA.: Moody Institute of Science), film script, 10.

2. Thomas J. Peters and Robert H. Waterman, Jr., *In Search of Excellence* (New York: Harper & Row, 1982), 119–55.

3. Ibid., 134.

4. Ibid.

5. Frank Lewis Dyer and Thomas Commerford Martin, *Edison: His Life and Inventions*, vol. 2 (New York: Harper & Brothers Publishers, 1910), 616.

6. Hugh Steven, *The Man with the Noisy Heart* (Chicago: Moody, 1979), 23.

7. Christopher Smart, *The Midwife: or, The Old Woman's Magazine* (London: Printed for Thomas Carnan, 1753), 37.

8. Stanley and Patricia Gundry, eds., *The Wit and Wisdom of D. L. Moody* (Grand Rapids: Baker, 1982), 64.

9. Steven, *The Man with the Noisy Heart*, 60.

10. Ibid., 65.

11. Fox, *Survivor Number Three*, 11.

12. Steven, *The Man with the Noisy Heart*, 69.

13. Ibid., 82.

14. Ibid., 99–100.

15. Ibid., 112.

16. Ibid., 125.

Chapter 5: Single-Mindedness—For a Lifetime

1. John Dryden, "Absalom and Ahithophel," 1681, Poetry Foundation, https://www.poetryfoundation.org/poems/44172/absalom-and-achitophel.

2. Thomas J. Peters and Robert H. Waterman, Jr., *In Search of Excellence* (New York: Harper & Row, 1982), 15.

3. Ibid.

Chapter 6: Love—The Mender of Souls

1. Richard Ellsworth Day, *Bush Aglow* (Philadelphia: Judson, 1936), 146.

2. George Verwer, *Come! Live! Die!* (Wheaton, IL: Tyndale, 1972), 20–21.

3. Ibid., 14.

4. Francis Schaeffer, *The Mark of the Christian* (Downers Grove, IL: InterVarsity, 1970), 13.

5. George Verwer, *A Revolution of Love* (Kansas City: Walterick, n.d.), 17.

6. Verwer, *Come! Live! Die!*, 14–15.

7. Verwer, *Revolution of Love*, 24–25.

8. Lawrence Tong, International Director, 2016 annual O.M. Ministry report.

Chapter 7: Suffering—The Refiner's Fire

1. M. R. DeHaan, *Broken Things: Why We Suffer* (1948; Grand Rapids: Discovery House Publishers, 1999), 66.

2. Ibid., 56.

3. Margaret Clarkson, *Grace Grows Best in Winter* (Grand Rapids: Zondervan, 1972), 35–36.

4. Edith Schaeffer, *Affliction* (Old Tappan, NJ: Revell, 1978), 111.

5. Fanny Crosby, *Memories of Eighty Years* (Boston: James H. Earle and Co., 1906), 19.

6. Ibid., 26.

7. Ibid., 171–72.

8. Walter C. Kaiser, *A Biblical Approach to Personal Suffering* (Chicago: Moody, 1982), 14.

Chapter 8: Prayer—The Lifeline to Heaven

1. E. F. and L. Harvey, *Kneeling We Triumph* (Blackburn, England: M.O.V.E. Press, 1971) 11; quoted in J. Oswald Sanders, *Prayer Power Unlimited* (Chicago: Moody, 1984), 49.

2. E. M. Bounds, *Power Through Prayer* (1910; repr., Chicago: Moody, 2009), 45–46.

3. Stanley and Patricia Gundry, eds., *The Wit and Wisdom of D. L. Moody* (Grand Rapids: Baker, 1982), 36.

4. Bounds, *Power Through Prayer*, 52.

5. Ibid.

6. Robert Cook, *Walk with the King Today* (Chappaqua, NY: Christian Herald, 1978), 26.

7. Bounds, *Power Through Prayer*, 17–18.

Chapter 9: Wisdom—The Eternal Perspective

1. Francis Schaeffer, *The Great Evangelical Disaster* (Westchester, IL: Crossway, 1984), 37.

2. Ibid., 51.

3. Ibid., 38.

Chapter 10: Staying Power—The Endurance to End Well

1. Russell H. Conwell, *Acres of Diamonds* (Old Tappan, NJ: Revell, 1960), 9–11.

2. Eugene Peterson, *A Long Obedience in the Same Direction* (Downers Grove, IL: InterVarsity, 1980), 11–12.

3. Mrs. Howard Taylor, *John and Betty Stam: A Story of Triumph*, rev. ed. (Chicago: Moody, 1982), 29.

4. Ibid., 119–20.

5. Ibid., 122–25.

Chapter 11: Steps of Excellence in the Life of D. L. Moody

1. J. Wilbur Chapman, *The Life and Work of Dwight L. Moody* (Philadelphia: Winston, E. Scull, 1900), 74–76.

2. Edward L. Pell, *D. L. Moody: His Life, His Work, His Words* (Richmond, VA: Johnson, 1900), 46.

3. James F. Findlay Jr., *Dwight L. Moody, American Evangelist: 1837–1899* (Chicago: University of Chicago Press, 1969), 77.

4. Arthur Percy Fitt, *Moody Still Lives* (Old Tappan, NJ: Revell, 1936), 21.

5. Ibid., 22.

6. Ibid., 22–23.

7. Ibid., 25.

8. William R. Moody, *The Life of D. L. Moody by His Son* (Old Tappan, NJ: Revell, 1900), 137–43.

9. Fitt, *Lives*, 26.

10. Findlay, *Dwight L. Moody*, 238.

11. Gundry, *Wit and Wisdom of Moody* (Grand Rapids: Baker, 1982), 63–64.

12. Fitt, *Lives*, 29.

13. Ibid.

14. D. L. Moody, *Glad Tidings: Comprising Sermon and Prayer-Meeting Talks Delivered at the N.Y. Hippodrome* (New York: E. B. Treat, 1876), 275–76; quoted in Findlay, *Dwight L. Moody*, 237.

15. John Pollock, *Moody, The Biography* (New York: McMillan, 1963), x.

16. Findlay, 132.

17. Ibid., 150.

18. Ibid., 150, 156.

19. "Men, Women and Events: Dwight L. Moody," *Cosmopolitan* 28 (March 1900): 510.

20. Ibid.

Chapter 12: Nineteenth-Century Heroes of Excellence

1. William Carey, "To Andrew Fuller" (August 14, 1804); quoted in Mary Drewery, *William Carey, A Biography* (Grand Rapids: Zondervan, 1979), 13.

2. Ibid., 16–17.

3. Richard Briscoe Cook, *The Wit and Wisdom of Rev. Charles H. Spurgeon* (New York: E. B. Treat, 1892), 31.

4. Ibid.

5. Ibid., 39–41.

6. Ibid., 50–52.

7. William Carey, *An Equiry into the Obligations of Christians to Use Means for the Conversion of the Heathens* (Leicester, England: Ann Ireland, 1792), 76; quoted in Drewery, *William Carey*, 38–39.

8. Ibid., 40.

9. Ibid., 119–21.

10. Ibid., 25.

11. Ibid., 154.

12. *Spurgeon, The People's Preacher* (Newcastle, England: Walter Scott, n.d.), 59–60.

13. Ibid., 62–64.

14. Ibid., 66.

15. Ibid., 77.

16. Richard Ellsworth Day, *The Shadow of the Broad Brim* (Philadelphia: Judson, 1934), 185.

17. Ibid., 227.

18. Walter Bruce David, *William Carey: Father of Modern Missions* (Chicago: Moody, 1963), 104–105.

Chapter 13: Present-Day Heroes of Excellence

1. Richard Ellsworth Day, *A Christian in Big Business* (Chicago: Moody, 1946), 38.

2. Ibid., 58–59.

3. Ibid., 64.

4. Ibid., 80.

5. Ibid., 81.

6. Ibid., 124.

7. Ibid., 161.

8. Ibid., 173.

9. Ibid., 148.

10. Ibid., 139.

11. Ibid., 140.

12. Gene Getz, *The Story of the Moody Bible Institute* (Chicago: Moody, 1969), 278.

13. Ibid., 163.

14. J. E. Haggai, *Success Secrets of the Bible* (Eugene, OR: Harvest House Publishers, 2013), 174–77.

15. "Haggai International," Charity Navigator, https://www
.charitynavigator.org/index.cfm?bay=search.summary&orgid=3792.

16. Joni Eareckson Tada, *Joni: An Unforgettable Story* (Grand Rapids: Zondervan, 2001).

STEPS TO PEACE WITH GOD

1. RECOGNIZE GOD'S PLAN—PEACE AND LIFE

The message in this book stresses that God loves you and wants you to experience His peace and life.

The BIBLE says, "For God so loved the world that He gave His only begotten Son, that whoever believes in Him should not perish but have everlasting life." *John 3:16, NKJV*

2. REALIZE OUR PROBLEM—SEPARATION FROM GOD

People choose to disobey God and go their own way. This results in separation from God.

The BIBLE says, "For all have sinned and fall short of the glory of God." *Romans 3:23, NKJV*

3. RESPOND TO GOD'S REMEDY—THE CROSS OF CHRIST

God sent His Son to bridge the gap. Christ did this by paying the penalty of our sins when He died on the cross and rose from the grave.

The BIBLE says, "But God shows his love for us in that while we were still sinners, Christ died for us." *Romans 5:8, ESV*

4. RECEIVE GOD'S SON—LORD AND SAVIOR

You cross the bridge into God's family when you ask Christ to come into your life.

The BIBLE says, "But to all who did receive him, who believed in his name, he gave the right to become children of God." *John 1:12, ESV*

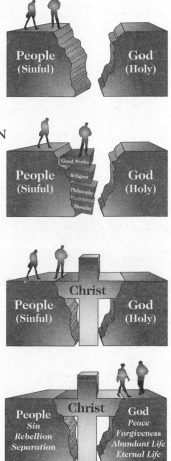

THE INVITATION IS TO:

REPENT (turn from your sins), ASK for God's forgiveness, and by faith RECEIVE Jesus Christ into your heart and life and follow Him in obedience as your Lord and Savior.

PRAYER OF COMMITMENT

"Dear God, I know that I am a sinner. I want to turn from my sins, and I ask for Your forgiveness. I believe that Jesus Christ is Your Son. I believe He died for my sins and that You raised Him to life. I want Him to come into my heart and to take control of my life. I want to trust Jesus as my Savior and follow Him as my Lord from this day forward. In Jesus' Name, amen."

If you are committing your life to Christ, please let us know!

Billy Graham Evangelistic Association
1 Billy Graham Parkway, Charlotte, NC 28201-0001
1-877-2GRAHAM (1-877-247-2426)
BillyGraham.org/commitment